Maverick Mothers

Epic Tales of Motherhood and the Making of the World's Most Successful People

Jamie Lillegard

STERLING
PRESS

© Copyright 2024 - All rights reserved.

0921 002
2 4 6 8 10 9 7 5 3
ISBN 978-3-98552-332-0

The content contained within this book may not be reproduced, duplicated or transmitted without direct written permission from the author or the publisher.

Under no circumstances will any blame or legal responsibility be held against the publisher, or author, for any damages, reparation, or monetary loss due to the information contained within this book, either directly or indirectly.

Legal Notice:

This book is copyright protected. It is only for personal use. You cannot amend, distribute, sell, use, quote or paraphrase any part, or the content within this book, without the consent of the author or publisher. No permission is required for biographies in this book as the subjects are public figures, all information is derived from publicly accessible sources, no likenesses are used, and it contains no defamatory content.

Disclaimer Notice:

The information contained within this document is for educational and entertainment purposes only. All effort has been executed to present accurate, up to date, reliable, complete information. No warranties of any kind are declared or implied. Readers acknowledge that the author is not engaged in the rendering of legal, financial, medical or professional advice. The content within this book has been derived from various sources.

Cover and interior images by Freepik.

Table of Contents

INTRODUCTION 1

CHAPTER 1: EVE BRANSON 7
    The Nurturer of Creativity 7
    Eve Branson's Journey and Influence 8
    Unleashing Imagination and Encouraging Risk-Taking......................9
    The Ripple Effect of Eve's Influence on Sir Richard Branson's Success 11
    Mentoring the New Manager..14

CHAPTER 2: IRMELIN INDENBIRKEN 17
    The Advocate of Environmental Consciousness..............................17
    Irmelin Indenbirken's Journey and Influence..................................18
    Inspiring Passion, Consciousness, and Responsibility 19
    The Ripple Effect of Irmelin's Influence on Leonardo DiCaprio's Success.....21
    A Heart Rising from the Ashes..23

CHAPTER 3: DELLSENA SPENCER 29
    The Breaker of Glass Ceilings..29
    Dellsena Spencer's Journey and Influence 30
    Removing Limitations and Glass Ceilings 31
    The Ripple Effect of Dellsena's Influence on Octavia Spencer's Success 33
    Where You Are Is Not Who You Are..35

CHAPTER 4: DELORIS JORDAN 39
    The Foundation of Greatness 39
    Deloris Jordan's Journey and Influence..40
    Cultivating Discipline and Resilience 42
    The Ripple Effect of Deloris' Influence on Michael Jordan's Success...............44
    Inspiration Lingers Long After the Final Buzzer 46

CHAPTER 5: ESTHER WOJCICKI 51
    Empowering Independence 51
    Esther Wojcicki's Journey and Influence 52
    Trust, Freedom, and Encouraging Autonomy 54
    The Ripple Effect of Esther's Influence on Susan Wojcicki's Success......56
    When Motherhood Is Just a Simple Trick.......................................58

CHAPTER 6: JACKIE BEZOS.. 61
    The Architect of Innovation..61
    Jackie Bezos' Journey and Influence...62
    Igniting Curiosity and Embracing Innovation 64

The Ripple Effect of Jackie's Influence on Jeff Bezos' Success 66
Listening to Children Is a Skill 68

CHAPTER 7: MARY LEE PFEIFFER 71
The Navigator of Dreams 71
Mary Lee Pfeiffer's Journey and Influence 73
Cultivating Passion and Perseverance 74
The Ripple Effect of Mary Lee's Influence on Tom Cruise's Success 76
Learning to Stand Up for Yourself 78

CHAPTER 8: BARIA ALAMUDDIN 81
Balancing Social Awareness and Personal Ambition 81
Baria Alamuddin's Journey and Influence 82
Love for Education That Transcended into a Battle for Human Rights 84
The Ripple Effect of Baria's Influence on Amal Clooney's Success 86
In Her Mother's Shoes 87

CHAPTER 9: CLARA JOBS 93
The Visionary Mentor 93
Clara Jobs' Journey and Influence 94
Fostering Creativity and Innovation 96
The Ripple Effect of Clara's Influence on Steve Jobs' Success 98
Breaking with Tradition to Create Innovative Things 99

CHAPTER 10: LEAH ADLER 103
The Maestro of Passion 103
Leah Adler's Journey and Influence 104
Inspiring Artistic Talent and Vision 105
The Ripple Effect of Leah's Influence on Steven Spielberg's Success 108
Guiding but Staying Open-minded 110

CHAPTER 11: MAYE MUSK 115
Balancing Passion and Purpose 115
Maye Musk's Journey and Influence 116
Encouraging Ambition and Embracing Challenges 118
The Ripple Effect of Maye's Influence on Elon Musk's Success 121
Musk and Rive – Twinning and Winning 122

CHAPTER 12: DEBBIE PHELPS 125
The Seeker of Success 125
Debbie Phelps' Journey and Influence 126
Guidance Through Obstacles to Stardom 127
The Ripple Effect of Debbie's Influence on Michael Phelps' Success 130
Being the Mother, Not the Coach 131

CHAPTER 13: PATRICIA NOAH 137
The Survivor of Adversities 137

Patricia Noah's Journey and Influence 139
Finding the Humor Together 141
The Ripple Effect of Patricia's Influence on Trevor Noah's Success 143
Overcoming Trauma with Determined Optimism 144

CHAPTER 14: ATA JOHNSON 149
The Angel in Human Form..149
Ata Johnson's Journey and Influence 150
The Sign of True Strength 151
The Ripple Effect of Ata's Influence on Dwayne Johnson's Success 154
Being the Rock that Moves Mars 155

CHAPTER 15: ADELE SANDBERG 161
Resilience and Growth 161
Adele Sandberg's Journey and Influence 163
Inspiring Change Despite Challenges 164
The Ripple Effect of Adele's Influence on Sheryl Sandberg's Success 165
Security and Growth from Humble Beginnings...166

CHAPTER 16: SONYA CARSON 173
Believing in Success 173
Sonya Carson's Journey and Influence 174
From Bad Report to Surgeon Extraordinaire 175
The Ripple Effect of Sonya's Influence on Ben Carson's Success 177
Learning at Home and Making Books a Priority..179

CONCLUSION 183

ABOUT THE AUTHOR 191

REFERENCES...193

Introduction

It's not easy being a mother. If it were, fathers would do it.

Dorothy Zbornak

I was six years old when my mother threw her drink at me. Luckily for me, she held on to the mug and her coffee had already gone cold, so I only had to deal with the discomfort of being wet. Of all the Christmas Days I've had in my life, that's the one I remember most.

You see, I was sitting on the sofa between my aunt and uncle, whining about some stupid small toy I didn't get for Christmas. Irritated by my petulance, my mom finally asked, "Did you have a good Christmas?" It was a rhetorical question. What she meant was, "Should you really be complaining right now after I bought you so many good presents?" And she had. She must've saved all year to afford those quality gifts for me and my brother. But my rebellious response to her question was, "NO." Barely a microsecond later, splash!

She was almost never angry at us, so it was quite a shock to see her react that way. Afterwards, my mother stormed out the room. My aunt and uncle, who miraculously stayed dry, just stared at me with raised eyebrows. I remember the only thing I felt at the time was embarrassment. Later on, I felt ashamed and deeply regretted upsetting the most important person in my life.

She raised us as a single mother, without any financial support from my father, who I've met maybe a handful of times since my parent's divorce when I was two. To provide for us, she worked long hours as a nursing assistant in a hospital an hour away from our house. Her job has many responsibilities, but on every shift she'll be turning patients over and washing them, cleaning up their vomit and poop, serving their meals, and bringing their medication. She'll do it all while dealing with their abuse, like it's her fault they smoked two packs a day and now had to have their leg amputated. I couldn't face most of what she does, but the thing that brings the biggest lump to my throat is when she tells me a patient she became close to dies on her shift. It's an emotionally draining job, and physically demanding for her skinny 5'3 frame, but she's still caring for her patients to this day at the age of 64.

Of course, it's only after I became an adult did I appreciate what my mother did to put food on the table and keep the electricity on. Being grateful was a lesson my developing mind had to instill in childhood for it to have a lasting impact on my life. That lesson came when I was six. But she didn't teach me about gratitude; her cold, milky beverage smacking me across the face said more than her words ever could have.

As you can see, tough love can prove to be valuable in inspiring healthy behaviors. This was also the case for Sir Richard Branson, whose mother kicked him out of the car for misbehaving and made him find his own way to his grandmother's house. He was around five years old at the time, but the experience has stayed with him throughout his life.

It was after hearing the story from Richard's childhood that I was reminded of my own. As I thought more about it, I wondered just how much events like those can influence a child and in what direction. If Richard can use what he learned from that traumatic event to go on to achieve incredible success, then is his success in spite of or thanks to the actions of his mother?

This question became the motivation to write this book.

In bite-sized chapters, I want to pull you into the lives of some of the most impactful and influential people today and give you a glimpse of how they were brought up. In particular, you'll learn how much of their greatness can be traced back to their maverick mothers.

I define a maverick mother as a mother who holds strong values and often uses unorthodox methods to power up key personality traits in her children, resulting in a person of an outstandingly independent, inventive mind, with the capacity, will, and perseverance to achieve greatness.

All of the successful people in this book have publicly praised their mothers for the role they played in their upbringing and how their level of success simply wouldn't have been possible had it not been for the mothers in their lives. My goal for this book is to tell you the stories that led up to the point when they so openly thanked their mothers.

The stories are real and told with respect.

Each chapter in this book is dedicated to a maverick mother. And each chapter is split into five sections as described below.

The first section introduces a larger-than-life individual who changed the world in their chosen field. It could be an entrepreneur, a movie star, a performer, an athlete, or someone in another profession, but for sure it's someone well-known and admired. This intro section ends with how the person has publicly acknowledged and celebrated the role their mother had in their life and career, setting the stage for the next section.

The second section is a short biography of the maverick mother. It summarizes as much information as I could gather about her life from the day she was born to the present time. It includes many important details, like her upbringing, her education, her interests, her marriage and children, her hardships, her successes and failures, and her impact on society.

Some stories are truly inspiring, some are extremely tragic, and some include very unbelievable things that really happened to them. From loves to losses, you'll get a behind-the-scenes look at the life of each mother and begin to understand the depth of her character. There's no mention of how she raised her famous child just yet—that's in section three—but I invite you to ponder how her journey through life could've developed her into the person responsible for many of her child's early triumphs and for laying the foundation for their future successes.

The third section paints a fuller picture of how each mother shaped the destinies of her offspring. Through many entertaining stories and anecdotes, you'll discover the key milestones and defining moments of their upbringing. It reveals how their experiences in childhood and adolescence positively affected them in later life.

One particular entertaining anecdote comes to mind. After watching his mother work on her many ventures and having lots of unsupervised time on his hands as a result, one of this book's stars started many business ventures of his own before adulthood. Like the time he and other teenage family members made it to the very last step in their planning application to open a new video arcade before being told by authorities that legally they were too young. Despite it happening four decades ago, his mother only found out about this secret project recently when it landed in the press. Today, his fearless approach in founding renowned global businesses has made him one the most successful entrepreneurs of all time.

Just to warn you though, not all stories are as inspiring as this one. While the eventual outcome of every person in this book is positive, the road to success for many was paved with difficulties like poverty, violence, illnesses, and death. Even the star from the story above went through incredible hardships in his early life, as did his mother.

By the time you finish this third section, I hope you feel more connected to the successful person and their mother beyond what you'd heard about them beforehand.

Of course, most of the mothers featured in this book have more than one child and in fact most of them are also successful in their own right. But in the interest of saving trees, I've stuck to how each of the mothers raised, inspired, and supported their most famous offspring.

The fourth section details the ripple effect of their mother's influence beyond individual achievements. Put another way, it describes how the person used a value or trait instilled in them by their mother to inspire positive change for many others. It's like a gift they've chosen to share with the wider community. It may not be the thing most people will remember them for, but for many, it's the thing they'd like most people to remember them for.

In many cases, this takes the form of philanthropy work. But it could also be a lesser-known achievement, such as when one of the changemakers in this book refused to let his industry die during the lockdowns and stay-at-home orders of the pandemic. His actions got everyone working again, making sure they could earn money to feed their families. As you'll read, his determination to do all he could to provide for his family came from a childhood mirroring his mother's work ethic.

The fifth and final section introduces other mothers that have had a similar impact on their children as the featured maverick and/or that have raised their offspring to become successful in the same field.

Without a shadow of a doubt, the other mothers featured in this fifth section deserved their own chapters. I simply couldn't find enough information about them or the way they raised their children to complete a full chapter and didn't want to shortchange you.

This book isn't a recipe for raising successful kids, but I've learned a lot from writing this book on how to be a better parent. And it turns out my wife was right (again. I seem to have a habit of only realizing she's right about things much later), that encouraging our girls to read more books gives them a higher chance of success later in life. I'll also be doing less for them. Sure, I can draw a (slightly) better unicorn than my seven-year-old, but it'll do more for her in the long run if she completes her drawings by herself. And I'm sure I'll survive not being needed so much. With that being said, I've done my best to summarize key takeaways and consistent themes in the book's conclusion.

I've used the term 'mother' throughout the book, with the odd use of 'mom' here and there. This choice was made for my international readers. It sounds a bit too formal in places, so I'd be delighted if you could read any instances of 'mother' as 'mom', 'mum', 'mama', or whatever affectionate term you use for mothers in your part of the world.

I also welcome you to skip around this book as you please. Each chapter stands alone, completely unrelated to any other, making it easy to relax into a mother's story and enjoy it in it's entirety without being overwhelmed.

Let me end by saying that I'm well aware of how impossible it is for a mother's influence to be the only thing responsible for their children achieving success. I firmly believe it's just as important to recognize the other individuals and the unique experiences that shaped the world's greatest overachievers. For example, Michael Jordan will tell anyone just how much of a positive influence his mother has been on his success, but he was also close to his late father and received a lot of great advice from him that helped Michael excel in sports.

But I chose mothers as the focus of this book, and so let's celebrate the moms!

Chapter 1:

Eve Branson

Kids certainly need a lot of love so they know you're behind them whatever they do, well, more or less.

Eve Branson

The Nurturer of Creativity

Some say success starts in childhood, where a child's mindset is shaped by that of their parents or closest caregivers. Sometimes, this can be in the form of a mother who takes a soft, caring approach to nurturing her children. Other times, teaching through a dose of tough love can be the ideal strategy to drive a child to success, as is evident in the case of Sir Richard Branson and his mother Eve. Many mothers have threatened to drop their children next to the road when they misbehave in the car, but Eve actually did that. That was a moment Richard believes that propelled him to strive for success in his life—an incredible journey with no end of hard work and dedication.

The story of Richard Branson is one of optimism, persistence, exploration, and creativity. There is no simple answer to the question, "Who is Sir Richard Branson?" On paper, he's a business mogul who founded the Virgin Group with interests in entertainment, aviation, and sports, to name a few. His entrepreneurial skills are so profound that he was knighted at Buckingham Palace in 2000. But he's more than that. He is also a son who loved and adored his mother so much that he wanted her to accompany him on most of his adventures.

Eve Branson's Journey and Influence

Born in London in 1924, Eve became successful in several different fields. She first served at the British Women's Royal Naval Service (WRENS), after which she took up ballet, became an airline hostess, and eventually established herself as a successful author. Although she wrote several books, her most prominent publication was her 2013 autobiography *Mum's the Word: The High-Flying Adventures of Eve Branson*. The subtitle of her book seems more fitting for her son, but Eve loved adventure and navigating the skies as much as Richard, once pretending to be a boy so she could take glider lessons.

During an interview with *The Guardian*, Eve explained that when Richard was a child, they had deep financial struggles. Her husband, Ted, failed his bar exams, and Eve had to find a way to earn an income for her young family, which included Richard's two sisters. Eve has spoken openly about the poverty that Richard grew up in. Being poor has pushed her to do whatever she could to make ends meet. However, she believes that knowing what it's like to struggle will only make you stronger as a person.

Her entrepreneurial spirit came through, and she started a factory in her back garden to make things like coverings for wastepaper baskets and table mats. She would then sell these products to Harrods, the luxury department store in London. She was, without a doubt, a fantastic role model of hard work, entrepreneurship, and creativity for Richard to learn from.

Before she died in 2021, Eve served on the board of directors for several non-profit organizations. Her legacy lives on through The Eve Branson Foundation, which she founded in 1998. The Foundation carries out philanthropic work and child welfare advocacy in the North African country of Morocco, a place and people she loved deeply.

Unleashing Imagination and Encouraging Risk-Taking

Eve was an encouraging mother but tried to be firm with her son, who could be extremely mischievous at times. "He was a tricky one to raise. There was something there, you felt he was a bit special so you couldn't be too cross with him," Eve told *The Guardian* (Day, 2014).

There were, however, times when even this maternal maverick's patience ran dry. When Richard was around five years old, they were traveling by car to his grandmother's house. He was being boisterous and demanding in the back seat, and Eve had had enough. As punishment, she stopped the car next to the road and forced him out: Young Richard would have to find the way to his grandmother's house all by himself. In a blog post, Richard described this as one of the most important moments of his childhood. The experience taught him that he needs to control his own emotions and rely on himself to get what he wants and needs. It also helped him to deal with his shyness, as he had no other choice but to ask passersby for directions to his grandmother's house.

His family's improving financial situation and his mother's entrepreneurial streak inspired Richard to try his hand at business at a young age, although at first, he failed more times than he succeeded. He first tried to grow Christmas trees in their backyard to sell over the holidays, but rabbits destroyed them. Then, he tried his luck at breeding parakeets, but when Richard went to boarding school, Eve got tired of looking after them and set them free.

Eve used these failed attempts to help Richard understand the value of learning from mistakes. In an interview with *Business Insider,* Richard described his mother as a loving and supportive person who always wanted the best for her children and would push them to reach their potential.

Richard continued to pursue his interests and business possibilities, with his big breakthrough coming at the direct hands of Eve. "It's no exaggeration to say I owe my career to Mum," he wrote in a blog (Branson, 2021b). It was back in the 1960s when Eve picked up a necklace lying on the road. She handed it in at the police station, but, when it hadn't been claimed after three months, the police told Eve she could have it. She sold the necklace for £100 and gave the money to Richard. This was the money he used to start Virgin, originally a mail-order record company, which would later expand to over 40 companies across five sectors of business on five different continents.

He gives his mother the credit for teaching him about business. Richard viewed Eve as the ultimate entrepreneur who would constantly look at creating her own small businesses to support her family. From mirroring Eve, Richard learned not just how to build and develop a company but also how to treat people, make the most of your creativity, and find a work-life balance.

Eve didn't fall short of talents, and her achievements show a great drive to pursue diverse interests throughout her working career. From her thoughts and recollections on parenting expressed in interviews and various publications, Eve states she was intent on allowing Richard to learn from experience while she provided space, time, and resources to follow through with his interests.

The ability to bounce back from challenges, adapt to new circumstances, and turn setbacks into opportunities became essential components of Richard's entrepreneurial journey. His remarkable strength in the face of business challenges and ability to accept responsibility for his own actions can, to a large degree, be attributed to the invaluable lessons instilled by his mother.

Eve's example shows how important it is for families to be open to creativity and learning. This is evident in the many business ventures Richard undertook during his teenage years before eventually starting the Virgin Group. Eve was by his side supporting him, helping him learn the necessary lessons through this experience, and being a good role model through her own businesses. Failure will happen, but a child who is raised to embrace creativity won't feel discouraged by it. Instead, they will enjoy the process itself, valuing their adventure a lot more than the result they expected to achieve.

In his blog on Virgin's website, Richard wrote that instead of mourning her loss, he wants to celebrate his mother for the amazing person she was and the incredible opportunities and love she gave others (2021a). And so, after her death, he named one of his planes after her, *The Fearless Lady*.

The Ripple Effect of Eve's Influence on Sir Richard Branson's Success

From setting up Virgin with a bit of found treasure to his adventures in space, there's a lot of Eve in every step Richard takes. Whether he's bouncing back from a business crisis or launching companies that literally aim for the stars, you can see his mother's influence. Eve taught him to get creative with what he's got and never give up—lessons he took to heart. Remember the necklace story? That's Eve's ingenuity and resourcefulness at play, and Richard has been living by those principles ever since. He's not scared to take risks or face challenges because Eve showed him that's just part of the adventure.

Eve obviously helped Richard make a success of his life, but Eve's life lessons also turned Richard into someone people look up to. He's not just a business mogul; he's a source of inspiration, showing that being nice and doing good aren't just for show. They're about making a real difference.

In Richard Branson's books, he chronicles his entrepreneurial journey and distills the principles that have guided his successful ventures, which resonate strongly with readers including notable figures like Stelios Haji-Ioannou, founder of easyGroup, Stacey Mayo, founder of Solutions By Stacey, and Michelle Mone, founder of Ultimo. His writings emphasize Eve's virtues of risk-taking and innovation, inspiring a broad spectrum of entrepreneurs to pursue their unique paths. Michelle Mone, for instance, illustrates the profound impact of Richard and Eve's philosophy. Coming from a challenging background in Glasgow, with early struggles and doubts due to dyslexia, Michelle found motivation in Richard's stories during her formative years. She has often expressed how a teenage fascination with Richard—a picture of Sir Richard Branson in place of the usual boy band poster most teen girls have on their wall—spurred her on to entrepreneurial success. She defied her initial academic setbacks to establish and grow Ultimo into a leading brand. Michelle's tribute to Richard as her "ultimate business hero" simply shows us the momentous part that role models, like Richard, can play in shaping the aspirations and careers of even those who face the most daunting obstacles.

Richard's influence extends far beyond the reach of his numerous literary works; he's a dynamic force on social media, particularly LinkedIn, where he shines as a true rockstar. He uses the professional network as a platform to actively encourage others to step up and make their mark. By urging his followers to take risks and chase their dreams, Richard becomes a catalyst for growth and innovation among budding entrepreneurs.

One poignant example of how Richard uses LinkedIn to amplify young entrepreneurs is the story of Angus Copelin-Walters, a young, dyslexic entrepreneur from Australia. Angus, at just 13 years old, founded Croc Candy and also serves as a passionate ambassador for Made By Dyslexia, a cause close to Richard's own advocacy for neurodiversity. Richard first met Angus in 2019 during a trip to Australia, and they have maintained a mentor-mentee relationship ever since. In a heartfelt post, Richard recounted their initial meeting and the subsequent entrepreneurship mentoring session where he shared valuable business advice with Angus. Like so many of Richard's posts, he doesn't take credit for shaping Angus' entrepreneurial journey but rather highlights Angus' achievements and celebrates the significant growth of Croc Candy over the years.

Through his posts on LinkedIn, Richard Branson boosts the profiles of emerging entrepreneurs like Angus, which inspires a vast network of professionals to support and engage with innovative young minds. His posts often lead to increased visibility, connections, and opportunities for these young entrepreneurs, illustrating the powerful role that Richard plays in nurturing the next generation of business leaders through social media.

Looking at the big picture, Richard Branson's journey is more than his achievements. It's about how Eve's wisdom helped him become someone who's not just successful but also genuinely inspiring. Through his actions, his encouragement of risk-taking and giving back, and his incredible reach on social media, Richard shows what success really means. It's about making a difference, spreading positivity, and, above all, staying true to the lessons learned from someone who believed in you from the start. Eve's legacy, through Richard, teaches us that real success is about how we influence the world and each other, proving that sometimes, the most impactful lessons come from home.

Mentoring the New Manager

To nurture kids who aspire to be entrepreneurs and risk-takers involves more than just encouragement—it's about setting a foundation of values and creativity that can guide them through the ups and downs of embarking on entrepreneurial ventures.

When Eve Branson taught Richard about business, she instilled in him values like integrity, flexibility, and compassion. These values become the backbone of good business practices as well as leading a fulfilling life. In fact, Richard Branson's story parallels that of Janice Bryant Howroyd, where both entrepreneurs were significantly influenced by their family values and their examples of perseverance and dedication.

Janice Bryant Howroyd's journey to becoming the first African-American woman to build a billion-dollar business is deeply rooted in the values and practices instilled by her parents. Raised in a large family in rural North Carolina, Janice credits her mother's managerial skills and the cooperative spirit she fostered at home as foundational to her success. Her mother ran the household like a tight ship, teaching her children the importance of organization, cooperation, and responsibility from a young age. These lessons proved invaluable as Janice navigated the complex world of entrepreneurship and business management.

Her mother's influence extended beyond practical household management. She emphasized the importance of education and building a purpose-driven life. These principles not only shaped Janice's personal ethos but also became the pillars of her business philosophy, influencing how she leads and grows her global enterprise. "My mama taught my 10 siblings and me that in order to be outstanding, you've got to be willing to stand out. And our dad taught us that together, we could win, so we could win with anything that we put our minds to," said Janice in an interview with Harvard Business Review as she reflected on the amazing spirit of her parents despite the extreme difficulties of growing up in a segregated society (Ignatius, 2023).

The stories of Richard Branson and Janice Bryant Howroyd illustrate the profound impact that strong maternal influences can have on entrepreneurial success. Eve Branson taught Richard the importance of perseverance and effort by encouraging him to take on challenges and supporting his ventures, no matter how unconventional. Similarly, Janice's mother instilled in her the values of organization, cooperation, and responsibility. Both mothers created environments where curiosity was nurtured and every idea considered, helping their children see opportunities where others saw obstacles. Their mothers' examples of using success to make a positive impact fostered not just successful entrepreneurs, but compassionate and ethical leaders committed to giving back to their communities.

Chapter 2:

Irmelin Indenbirken

My mom, Irmelin, taught me the value of life. Her own life was saved by my grandmother during World War II.

Leonardo DiCaprio

The Advocate of Environmental Consciousness

Picture a Hollywood icon who once captured hearts as a doomed lover on a sinking ship and now fights to save our planet from meeting its own doom. This award-winning actor is just as well-known for his unforgettable performances as he is for his relentless environmental advocacy. Leonardo DiCaprio is one of the best-known actors in modern Hollywood. He's won dozens of accolades for distinguished roles in many highly esteemed movies, becoming a household name around the world. Who can forget his riveting performance as the charming con artist in *Catch Me If You Can*, the dream-hopping thief in

Inception, the audacious stockbroker in *The Wolf of Wall Street*, and of course his gritty, Oscar-winning role in *The Revenant*?

Whenever he's taking a break from being a Hollywood A-list actor, he's occupying the role of influential environmentalist and the founder of a foundation that works on preserving vulnerable ecosystems across the globe. His mother, Irmelin Indenbirken, has played a major role in her son's growth and success as both an actor and environmentalist. She is so important to Leonardo that on top of mentioning her specifically in his acceptance speeches, he actually named a newly discovered snake species after her.

Irmelin Indenbirken's Journey and Influence

To say that Irmelin had a difficult upbringing won't do justice to what this maternal maverick had to endure in her life. She was born in 1943 in an air raid shelter in Germany during World War II. While the thoughts of bombs going off around an innocent baby would be harrowing enough for most people, that's not where Irmelin's struggles ended. When she was just a toddler, she broke her leg and had to go to hospital where she had to fight for her life after contracting several serious illnesses.

During an interview with *People*, Leonardo explained that the hospital was filled with soldiers and refugees from the war. As a result of overfull hospital wards, Irmelin contracted half a dozen serious illnesses and remained in hospital for almost three years. Since the nurses were inundated with patients, Leonardo's grandmother had to take over the caring duties to nurse Irmelin back to health. "When you see a picture of my mother, it's heartbreaking. It brings tears to my eyes knowing what she's been through in her life," Leonardo once reflected (Quihuiz, 2023b).

When Irmelin was 12 years old, she and her family moved across the Atlantic Ocean and settled in New York. After completing school, she worked as a secretary and attended City College. It was here where she met George DiCaprio. Not long after they started dating, the couple found out that Irmelin was pregnant. They decided to move to Los Angeles in the hopes of giving their child a better life.

Unfortunately, the couple struggled financially and had to settle in a part of the city that Leonardo describes as "a rough area" in East Los Angeles. There was a major prostitution ring on the street corner close to his house, and crime and violence were the order of the day (Quihuiz, 2023b). Only a year after Leonardo was born, George and Irmelin called time on their relationship.

Inspiring Passion, Consciousness, and Responsibility

No matter how you look at Irmelin and her influence on Leonardo's life, it's very clear that she did everything she could to provide her son with the best life she could give him, whatever their circumstances. She even put her own needs aside to work with her ex-husband to perfect the art of co-parenting. To do this, Irmelin and George decided to become neighbors to ensure that Leonardo would have the presence of both his parents in his life and never feel neglected.

While many children thrive on continuously going on exciting adventures, Leonardo was happy living the more monotonous lifestyle his mother could afford. Leonardo actually appreciated the repetitiveness of his life as this helped him to truly remember everything his mother did for him. "We did the same things—went to the same museums, took the same pony rides—and those things have become locked in my memory as one good experience" (Quihuiz, 2023b). His parents never tried to go out of their way to show him a good time or expose him to the fabulous side of life. Just being there was enough for young Leo.

When it came to education, however, Irmelin wanted better for Leonardo. She simply wasn't going to allow the difficult neighborhood they lived in to keep her son from excelling in life. Instead, she decided to put Leonardo in a school on the other side of the big city and drove for three hours every day to take him to and from school. Going to school in a better neighborhood gave Leonardo a chance to see another side of life and that opportunities are accessible even to people living in what he dubbed "prostitution alley".

Leonardo was only 12 years old when he started dreaming of having a career in show business. Up to this point, he had only appeared in commercials. When he told Irmelin about his aspirations, she supported him completely, which is all the more remarkable given that he decided to drop out of high school to accomplish his dream. Without questioning him or his big dreams, she made the effort to find out about different auditions he could try out for and drove him to them whenever she could. "She's the only reason I'm able to do what I do," Leonardo explained during an interview (Whitman, 2022). He got his first major role aged 16 when he played Luke in the TV sitcom *Growing Pains*, and the rest is history.

Once Leonardo made it big, Irmelin wasn't just a bystander or supporter from the side. She can be seen in small, background roles in many of his movies, including *Total Eclipse*, *The Beach*, and *Blood Diamond*. She even sat in the executive producer's chair in the 2007 movie *The 11th Hour*, a documentary film about the state of the natural environment and possible solutions to improve it.

Even with the success he has achieved, he has never forgotten the sacrifices Irmelin made in raising her talented son. During his acceptance speech for the Actors Inspiration Award at the 30th anniversary of the Screen Actors Guild Foundation, he thanked his mother for the role she played in shaping the person he has become, the actor he has become, as well as the philanthropic efforts he has dedicated a large portion of his life to.

After working on arguably one of his biggest roles in *Titanic*, Leonardo was inspired by fellow environmentalist and director James Cameron to play his part in protecting the earth. Leonardo then met with Vice President Al Gore to discuss the urgent threat of climate change. Later that same year, Irmelin and Leonardo co-founded the Leonardo DiCaprio Foundation (LDF), an organization aiming to protect key species and fragile ecosystems, and, as such, foster a healthy relationship between nature and humanity.

The Ripple Effect of Irmelin's Influence on Leonardo DiCaprio's Success

Just imagine how proud Irmelin must be when she sees the kind of person Leonardo has become and the amazing impact he's had on the world around him. Because beyond the accolades and traditional measures of success an actor achieves, he's out there actually trying to make positive change happen. And it's in Leonardo's dedication to making the world a bit brighter for the next generation that we see just how much Irmelin's legacy is woven into his character and compassionate worldview.

At just 24 years old, a year after the release of the blockbuster film *Titanic*, Leonardo began his journey as an environmental advocate when he and Irmelin founded the aforementioned Leonardo DiCaprio Foundation. Over the years, the LDF has awarded grants totaling more than $100 million to support projects across all oceans and continents. From preserving wild tiger populations in Nepal to protecting lowland gorillas in Central Africa and snow leopards in Asia, the LDF has made a tangible impact on biodiversity conservation efforts worldwide.

Leonardo and Irmelin have also leveraged his fame, influence, and knowledge of the entertainment industry to raise awareness about environmental issues on a global scale. In 2011, Irmelin showcased her production skills in the documentary *The 11th Hour*, which featured over 50 experts—scientists, academics, and public figures—who delve into the critical challenges our world is grappling with today. These specialists uncover how human activities have been harming the Earth's intricate natural systems and propose possible solutions to either undo or mitigate this damage before it's too late to preserve our planet. Leonardo produced, co-wrote, and narrated the documentary.

Other notable credits include the 2014 documentary film *Cowspiracy: The Sustainability Secret* as executive producer. In 2016, he also narrated and produced the documentary *Before the Flood*, which explored the devastating consequences of climate change at a crucial time when the world seemed to be shifting its priorities.

In 2014, the United Nations appointed Leonardo as a Messenger of Peace. Although this role entails him focusing predominantly on climate change, it's undeniable that Irmelin's upbringing in a war-ridden Germany inspired his drive to want to bring peace to all aspects of humanity. While Irmelin's war was between nations, the war that Leonardo fights is between man and nature.

In 2019, Leonardo and Irmelin took a bold step forward by integrating the LDF's staff and operations into Earth Alliance. This strategic move brought together the expertise and resources of the LDF, Emerson Collective, and Global Wildlife Conservation, creating a powerful collaborative platform to tackle pressing environmental challenges with renewed vigor and optimism.

In the digital age, Leonardo has harnessed the power of social media to educate his millions of followers about environmental issues and inspire action. His online accounts shed light on threats to biodiversity, Indigenous peoples' climate leadership, and the devastating consequences of activities like planned drilling in the Okavango River Basin of southern Africa.

Through his foundation, Leonardo was given the opportunity to name a new snake species found in Panamanian jungles in South America, he immediately decided to honor his mother whom he calls the most important woman in his life. The red and orange tree snake is now known as the *Sibon irmelindicaprioae*, or Irmelin DiCaprio's Snail-eating Snake (Eyewitness News, 2023). What a fitting way to immortalize his affection for his favorite woman.

Irmelin is never far behind her successful son when he continues to do his bit to preserve the environment. In fact, her contribution to their foundation is so astounding that TreePeople, one of the largest environmental organizations based in California, gave her the Evergreen Award in 2023 for her tireless work.

As the world grapples with the escalating climate crisis and the urgent need to protect biodiversity, Leonardo DiCaprio reminds us that individual actions can make a positive change. And at the heart of his journey lies the enduring influence of his mother, Irmelin Indenbirken, whose legacy continues to ripple outward, inspiring others to take up the mantle of environmental stewardship.

A Heart Rising from the Ashes

The story of Leonardo and Irmelin's journey is remarkably similar to that of another Oscar winner-mother duo in many ways.

Best known for playing the roles of charismatic antagonists, Joaquin Phoenix is able to embrace and fully immerse his performance in layers of experiences that portray people whose actions are considered harmful and destructive. He brings a certain uniqueness of performance to the table, which helped him shape an authentic style of acting expression that's distinguishable regardless of the role he plays.

When you look at his early life, it's clear that he had numerous experiences to draw inspiration from. As if it wasn't already traumatic enough that he and his family were part of a Christian cult that exploited young children for sex, he also witnessed the tragedy of his older brother dying from a drug overdose right in front of him. He was the one who made the frantic call to 911 for help.

His early life challenges, deeply intertwined with family dynamics, set the stage for a career defined by intense and captivating performances. Throughout his tumultuous life, his mother, Arlyn "Heart" Phoenix was always there, supporting his individuality and authenticity, protecting her five children as best she could, and celebrating their growth.

Born in the Bronx, New York, in 1944, Arlyn Sharon Dunetz grew up in a family of Jewish immigrants, with her mother originally from Hungary and her father from Russia. Although her family celebrated all the Jewish holidays, they never attended synagogue. Once she finished school, she married a computer programmer and worked as a secretary. However, when she turned 24 years old, she grew so tired of her life that she left her husband and New York and hitchhiked to California. Arlyn explained that she lost her individuality and zest for life and knew that she had to make changes to get that back. She knew she had to take charge of her own life to become the person she was destined to be.

While hitchhiking, she met her second husband, songwriter John Lee Bottom, with the couple getting married the following year. After the birth of their first two children, they joined a Christian sect, Children of God, and became missionaries. As a result of their laid-back style of living and the work they did in the sect, they moved around a lot. This resulted in their five children being born in different countries or American states. Joaquin, their third child and second son, was born in Puerto Rico, and they chose his name to fit in with his country of birth.

The names of their other children—River, Rain, Summer, and Liberty—fit with the couple's hippy existence.

Eventually, the couple grew suspicious of the sect they were part of. They illegally boarded a cargo ship to escape and bring their children back to America. After arriving back in America, the couple changed their surname to Phoenix, referencing the mythical bird rising from the ashes. Arlyn got a job as the assistant of a casting manager at NBC, which provided the perfect foundation for Joaquin to launch his career in show business.

Working for a major television network, Arlyn, who also went by the name Heart, found herself in the middle of Hollywood's talent pool and could guide her children on making good choices to develop their careers in the industry. Her networking landed her children contracts with a well-known casting agent Iris Burton. In starting his career, Joaquin decided to use a stage name Leaf, as he felt this would better match the names of his siblings.

This wasn't Joaquin's first taste of the performing arts. While they were still traveling with the sect, Arlyn and her husband didn't earn a formal income. They relied on picking fruit or doing odd jobs to feed their young children. On days they couldn't find any work or food to eat, their children would perform and sing on street corners for donations to buy food: the better the performance, the more money they would get. This showed Joaquin the power that lay within him and his creative expression. It is this sense of individuality and willingness to do what you can to entertain others that would later become the aspect of his acting that set him apart from his peers in Hollywood.

Being part of the sect also taught Joaquin the importance of being critical of your environment and standing up for what you believe in. It later emerged that the sect was actually a cult that groomed and exploited young children sexually. Joaquin's older brother River spoke openly about losing his virginity at only four years old during their time at the cult (Koehler & Paris, 2023). The FBI and New York Attorney's Office investigated the claims of sexual abuse made against the cult. Arlyn and John were never implicated in any wrongdoing.

Joaquin has spoken out about the cult and his parent's involvement and said that his parents were often considered to be guilty through their association with the cult. However, he believes they were innocent victims of the whole affair, as they truly believed in the good they believed the sect could bring. His parents thought they'd found a community of like-minded people who could support each other and share similar values and ideals. Joaquin says that the moment his parents realized that everything wasn't as they appeared to be in the sect, they took their children and got out. "Cults rarely advertise themselves as such," he explains (Bueno, 2014). In doing so, Arlyn taught her children the importance of listening to their inner voices and removing themselves from situations that might be harmful, if not immediately, then as soon as possible.

Joaquin was only three years old when they left the sect. It was on the boat trip from Venezuela back to the United States that Joaquin and his family made the collective decision to become vegans. This was after watching the fishermen catch and violently kill the fish. Joaquin had a strong reaction to witnessing what he felt to be a great injustice. It made him angry and distrustful of humanity. "I think that during that moment we knew that we were not going to eat meat anymore," Joaquin recalled during a interview (Koehler & Paris, 2023).

Arlyn's influence on her children's lives stretched further than just being aware of their environments. Since she worked closely with many big names in Hollywood, she had a direct impact on Joaquin and his siblings' careers. His older sister, Rain, also an actress, spoke openly about this and says that Arlyn got to know both the positives and negatives of Hollywood, and could warn her children of the bad aspects and guide them to experience the beautiful things this industry can offer. "It was almost like having an insider," Rain said Arlyn would spend countless hours rehearsing lines with her children and driving them to and from castings and acting gigs. The only thing she didn't allow her children to do was commercials for junk food, meat, and milk (Corner, 2011). Arlyn's insider knowledge of Hollywood allowed her to effectively navigate its challenges and opportunities, ensuring her children could thrive without compromising their integrity.

The eldest of the siblings, River Phoenix, was the first to make it as an actor. However, on the night of Halloween in 1993, when he was only 23 years old, he overdosed in the nightclub Viper Room. Joaquin was with his brother at the time and called 911 for help. Unfortunately, by the time the emergency services arrived at the club, they couldn't save River's life.

The death of his brother was difficult for Joaquin and his family to deal with. They moved to Costa Rica to mourn. Shortly after that, Arlyn and John separated. During this time, Arlyn continued to motivate her children to not allow their lives to end with River's passing. When Joaquin eventually returned to acting, he ditched the name Leaf, and his career really took off. Arlyn also co-founded the River Phoenix Center for Peacebuilding, an organization that focuses on bringing peace to people living in difficult circumstances.

Even though her children achieved great success in Hollywood, Arlyn made it clear that there should never be any form of competition between them. Instead, she helped her children to share in their success and understand that every one of them would get their opportunity to shine, although it would seldom be at the same time. As Rain explained during an interview, their parents gave up many things in life to help their children go after their dreams. "My parents really were very dedicated to us. It was an incredibly selfless act" (Corner, 2011).

Like Leonardo, Joaquin is a vocal advocate for animal rights, environmental sustainability, and social justice. His activism is deeply personal and driven by early life experiences. Again, like Leonardo, he has narrated influential documentaries, including *Earthlings* and *Dominion*, which expose the various ways humans exploit animals for food, clothing, entertainment, and scientific research.

Filled with the strength and determination of surviving traumas in their lives, Irmelin and Arlyn went on to raise two of the world's most influential actors and environmental crusaders. Upon discovering their talents at an early age, they gave their sons support in finding phenomenal success in the industry—an impactful journey that's very much still unfolding.

Chapter 3:

Dellsena Spencer

My mom was very practical. She never, ever restricted our dreams, always told us we could do or be anything. Then I said, "Maybe I want to be an actor." And she said, "Maybe not that."

Octavia Spencer

The Breaker of Glass Ceilings

The journey from obscurity to stardom is often paved with the silent sacrifices and lessons of our forebears, shaping not just careers but the very essence of who we become. Octavia Spencer is a well-known and respected American actress who has won a long list of awards, including a prestigious Academy Award. However, Octavia's childhood was anything but a fairytale.

Raised in a small house with six siblings and a mother who worked as a domestic worker, the family lived in poverty. Despite their conditions, Octavia's mother, Dellsena, always made sure her daughters had everything they needed, which was mostly things she herself didn't have as a child.

Even though Dellsena Spencer died before her daughter made it big in Hollywood, the life lessons she taught Octavia helped shape her daughter as a person and an actress. In fact, it was Dellsena's life story that inspired Octavia not just to accept the role of a maid on *The Help*, but also contributed to her Oscar award-winning acting performance. Octavia was uniquely able to tap into the emotions and struggles of her character, bringing an authenticity to her performance that resonated with audiences around the world. Dellsena's legacy is a powerful reminder that what we provide for our children can transcend material wealth, shaping their character and ambitions and helping them to achieve success in their own lives.

Dellsena Spencer's Journey and Influence

Dellsena was a woman who faced countless challenges in her life, but she never let those obstacles define her. Born in 1945 in Montgomery, Alabama, she grew up in extreme poverty and had very limited career options, so she worked as a maid in people's houses. However, she soon realized that this job wouldn't earn her a big enough salary to support herself and her seven daughters. As a single mother, she had no one to rely on to help her raise or financially support her daughters. Dellsena started doing as many odd jobs as she could fit into her day, which often meant that she would only get home to her daughters late at night. She was perpetually exhausted but held firm to her determination to keep going.

As if having her hands full providing for and raising her seven daughters wasn't demanding enough, she also had to help Octavia overcome her challenges with dyslexia. With limited time available, Dellsena still managed to work closely with Octavia's teacher to help her daughter find ways to cope with letters that seemed to jump around on the page. She knew that education was the key to a better future, and she was willing to do whatever it took to ensure that her children had the opportunities they deserved.

Dellsena passed away when Octavia was only 18 years old. Although Octavia was interested in acting as a child, she wanted a more practical career that would provide her with more financial stability than her mother had. She opted to go to Auburn University, where she obtained her bachelor's degree in English. After that, she worked at a small casting company in Alabama. Octavia tried her luck by auditioning for a small role in the thriller *A Time to Kill*. She got the role, followed by many other smaller roles to launch her career.

Octavia has publicly spoken about her mother's influence in preparing her for Hollywood. Dellsena's teachings on breaking through societal limitations echo through Octavia's approach to life and her career, which helped to lay the necessary foundation for Octavia to build her successful acting career on. "I think you have to have blind faith in yourself and your ability" (Petit, 2016). Octavia's reflections on her mother's influence serve as a reminder of the importance of instilling a belief in boundless potential in young people. With hard work and determination, anything is possible.

Removing Limitations and Glass Ceilings

In raising her daughters, Dellsena did whatever she could to protect them from bigotry and racism, to teach them to stand up for themselves, and to encourage them to always go for what they want.

During an interview, Octavia spoke about the significant impact that her mother's limitless beliefs have had on her life. She said that her very strong mother raised her and her sisters with the belief that the only limitations they had in their lives were the ones they created for themselves. "She taught us there was no glass ceiling. You have to not see boundaries. You have to see the sky is the limit, otherwise you will never get off the ground" (Petit, 2016). This enduring appreciation speaks volumes about the depth of Dellsena's impact on her daughter's life and worldview.

Even though her mother never saw her daughter achieve acting success, the life lessons her mother taught them as well as her sacrifices are something Octavia still values. Dellsena taught her daughter to take advantage of all the opportunities that come their way. "We had more than she did, and a lot less than a lot of people, even to this day. She is the one woman that I credit everything to," Octavia said (Desiree O, 2021)

Her mother's influence on Octavia's performance in *The Help*, arguably her best role to date and one that resulted in her winning an Oscar, is undeniable. In this movie, Octavia portrays the role of a maid working for a rich and often racist family. However, as was the case in Dellsena's life, Octavia's character didn't just accept her circumstances but believed she, and all the other maids, were much more than their employers might have believed. "The woman who has inspired me the most is my mother. I am a product of her disadvantages in life," Octavia told *People* (Guglielmi, 2018). Through her role, Octavia pays homage to her mother, bringing Dellsena's spirit to the screen.

She honored her mother in 2017 when her movie, *Hidden Figures*, was released. It deals with the racial and gender discrimination many women have to deal with on a daily basis. To help spread the message of the film and show her support for women who raised their children alone, much like her own mother had to do, Octavia booked out the entire movie theater in Baldwin Hills, California, and invited all disadvantaged women and children to watch the movie free of charge. "My mom would not have been able to afford to take me and my siblings. So, I'm honoring her and all single parents," she explained (Rossi, 2017). With this gesture of remembrance and solidarity, Octavia bridges her personal history with her public achievements.

The importance of family and the wisdom of maternal advice remain constant sources of strength for Octavia.

Till today, Octavia relies on her family, and, when she needs advice, she would turn to them but also think of what her mother would've done in the same situation. Dellsena also instilled the importance of spending time with her family, particularly on big occasions. "I've always spent Christmas with my family. Until I get married, I'll always spend Christmas with my family in Alabama," Octavia said (Desiree O, 2021). Dellsena's teachings on family and resilience continue to guide Octavia, echoing the timeless value of maternal wisdom. In the world of Hollywood glitz and glamour, Octavia Spencer's story stands out as a beacon of hope.

The Ripple Effect of Dellsena's Influence on Octavia Spencer's Success

A mother's wisdom and heart can leave a lasting imprint more powerful than making it big. Dellsena taught Octavia how to face life's ups and downs, and infused Octavia's spirit with grit, kindness, and a deep sense of purpose. This story beautifully showcases how the essence of a mother's teachings can spread, starting with her children who, as you're about to see, then pay it forward and inspire communities and future generations.

From the backdrop of her mother's teachings and the sacrifices she witnessed, Octavia Spencer emerged as a celebrated actress and a visionary committed to reshaping the narrative landscape of Hollywood.

Her role in *The Help*, while a tribute to the struggles faced by women like her mother, was just the beginning of a broader campaign to foster inclusivity and representation in film.

Octavia's understanding of diversity in Hollywood is deeply personal and influenced by what her mother instilled in her. Reflecting on her ambitions beyond acting, Octavia revealed, "In the past, I have said that my dream role is not a character or a figure from history. My dream role is that of a producer–a woman behind the scenes–who creates roles for diversity in films. I want to help create an industry that demonstrates what our society is as a whole" (Spencer, Interview).

Octavia's transition into production is a strategic move to cultivate a film industry that mirrors the real demographic fabric of society—a commitment that extends beyond African-American stories. She advocates for a cinema that encompasses all ethnicities and experiences, understanding that true change in Hollywood must transcend singular narratives. This perspective reveals her comprehensive vision for a multicultural narrative approach that challenges and dismantles longstanding stereotypes.

Understanding the dual nature of her industry as both art and business, Octavia emphasizes the importance of producing content that is inclusive but at the same time also engaging and commercially viable. "I want the movies I create [as an executive producer] to show a broader spectrum of the world–in all shapes, sizes, and religions–but at the same time also be compelling and interesting stories that the audience wants to watch. It is called show business after all!" (Spencer, Interview). Through this lens, she approaches her role as a producer with a pragmatic optimism, aiming to strike a balance between cultural representation and mainstream appeal.

Beyond her professional achievements, Octavia's actions speak to a legacy of empowerment inspired by her mother's life. Her initiative to screen *Hidden Figures* for disadvantaged women and children is a poignant example of how she uses her platform to honor her roots and uplift others. This gesture paid homage to Dellsena and reinforced the message that every individual deserves to see themselves represented in the stories told on the big screen.

Through her work, Octavia Spencer has transformed the narrative landscape of Hollywood, ensuring that the echoes of her mother's teachings resonate in the corridors of power. By championing diversity and pushing for more inclusive storytelling, she honors her mother's legacy and paves the way for future generations to envision a world without ceilings, just as Dellsena taught her to see the sky as the limit. In doing so, Octavia exemplifies how the influence of a single individual can inspire change that ripples through society, redefining what's possible in an industry often resistant to change.

Where You Are Is Not Who You Are

As parents and caregivers, we often get caught up in the material aspects of providing for our children. We focus on providing the latest gadgets, the trendiest clothes, and the fanciest toys. However, it's important to remember that true wealth lies in the intangible things we provide for our children.

It goes without saying that absolutely no child should ever experience extreme poverty, or any adult for that matter. But whether a child grows up in severe destitution or in more comfortable circumstances, the right environment and appropriate guidance can inspire that child towards remarkable success. For some, success may be measured by academic achievements, while for others, like the magnificent Dellsena and Octavia Spencer, it may be measured by personal growth, creativity, and community service.

Dellsena Spencer's life provides a compelling blueprint for nurturing ambition and a strong moral compass amidst challenging circumstances.

Facing the daily struggles of not having much, Dellsena emphasized the importance of education and creative problem-solving. She worked closely with Octavia's teachers to overcome her dyslexia, demonstrating that investing time and effort into educational support pays off, sometimes in bigger ways than you can ever imagine.

Dellsena's unyielding spirit in the face of hardship showed her daughters that self-belief is paramount. She embodied the principle that a person's circumstances don't define their future. Teaching kids to believe in their potential, as Dellsena did, can empower them to transcend their current conditions. But Dellsena's life lessons went beyond survival; they included instilling values of integrity and empathy. Her example of hard work, coupled with her dedication to treating others with respect and kindness, serves as a powerful model.

Although tremendously powerful, the story of Dellsena Spencer's maternal influence is not unique. Ursula Burns, the first Black female CEO of a Fortune 500 company, credits her rise to her mother, Olga Racquel Burns, a Panamanian immigrant who raised her children in a New York City housing project with a meager income. Like Dellsena Spencer, Olga emphasized education, hard work, and the belief that her children could achieve anything despite their circumstances. Ursula's journey from an intern to the CEO of Xerox was fueled by her mother's insistence on education and her internal drive, proving that "where you are is not who you are," a mantra that Ursula lived by throughout her career.

Both Ursula Burns and Octavia Spencer's narratives highlight the critical role mothers can play in shaping the destinies of their children. The environments that Ursula and Octavia grew up in were challenging, yet their mothers managed to create nurturing sub-environments that fostered growth and learning. They demonstrate how, even in the face of poverty and systemic obstacles, the lessons of perseverance, the value of education, and the belief in your potential can lead to groundbreaking success.

In a lighter sense, think of Ursula and Octavia's stories as examples of how even in the most unlikely gardens, with the right care and encouragement, the most beautiful flowers can bloom. Their mothers' influences were like sunlight and water to seeds, enabling them to grow into towering trees in their respective fields.

Chapter 4:

Deloris Jordan

My mother is my root, my foundation. She planted the seed that I base my life on, and that is the belief that the ability to achieve starts in your mind.

Michael Jordan

The Foundation of Greatness

From the basketball court to the boardroom, this iconic figure absolutely dominated his sport while transforming challenges into stepping stones for success and inspiring countless individuals along the way. He successfully broke free from the shackles of disadvantage and challenges to become arguably the greatest basketball player of all time. The man whose legacy in sports is just the tip of the iceberg, he continues to influence and uplift generations beyond the game. No one could deny that Michael Jordan's incredible achievements in sports, business, and philanthropy are a thing of wonder. Michael symbolizes excellence and determination and is an excellent role model for many young children hoping to use sports to break out of their circumstances.

Had it not been for the unrelenting support from his mother, Deloris Johnson, who was always showering her son with love, support, and encouragement, his life story likely would've read vastly different. Deloris, or Mother Jordan, as she is often referred to, homed in on each of her children's unique skills, helped them believe in themselves, and fulfilled the role of both mother and father after her husband was tragically killed.

Deloris Jordan's Journey and Influence

Deloris was born in 1941 in North Carolina. She met her husband, James Raymond Jordan, at a basketball game at their high school. James asked her father's permission to take his daughter out on a date, and from that first date, Deloris and James were inseparable. They got married just three years later.

With James involved in the Air Force after high school, the couple moved around a lot in just a few short years. After a brief stint in Texas, they welcomed the first of their children while in Virginia. When their second came along, James decided to leave the Air Force and moved the family to New York where he trained to become a mechanic and Deloris worked as a bank teller. They finally settled back in North Carolina less than ten years after graduating high school.

The couple had five children together, with Michael being their fourth. He has two older brothers, James Jr. (affectionately known as Ronnie) and Larry, an older sister Deloris, and a younger sister Roslyn. The five siblings spent the majority of their childhood in Wilmington, North Carolina, on a five-acre property. It was in that backyard where the Jordan siblings played, and where Michael's legendary competitive nature first emerged. Just ask Michael's brothers who'd often have to deal with his wrath whenever they beat him.

Deloris placed a high focus on her children's studies, believing that education drives children to learn how to improve themselves independently and therefore makes anything possible. She also placed high value in involving her children in activities at the church. Being part of the community taught Michael and his siblings valuable lessons, but mostly it kept them out of trouble while Mom and Dad were at work.

As Michael rose to stardom in the basketball arena, Deloris started to give back to their communities. She co-founded the Michael Jordan Foundation, through which money is raised for disadvantaged children, the James R. Jordan Foundation, founded after James was shot and killed while sleeping in his car at a highway rest stop, and the Kenya Women and Children's Wellness Center in Nairobi, Kenya.

Deloris Jordan is also an acclaimed author, penning a few children's books that have garnered widespread acclaim. Her most notable works include *Salt in His Shoes: Michael Jordan in Pursuit of a Dream*, co-authored with Michael's sister Roslyn. This inspirational book tells the story of young Michael's dreams of becoming a basketball star, emphasizing the values of patience, hard work, and faith. Another popular title is *Did I Tell You I Love You Today?*, also written by the mother-daughter duo and beautifully illustrated by Shane W. Evans, which explores the daily affirmations of love between a parent and child, capturing the tender moments that strengthen their bonds.

Deloris's contributions to literature extend beyond children's books. She's the author of a well-regarded parenting book, *Family First: Winning the Parenting Game*, first published in 1996. This book outlines her seven principles of effective parenting, drawing from her rich experience raising five children, including her renowned son. The book provides practical advice on fostering a supportive and nurturing home environment, emphasizing the importance of discipline, love, and family values.

With so many popular books to her name, it's easy to see Deloris's commitment to sharing the wisdom and values that have been instrumental in her family's success.

Cultivating Discipline and Resilience

While raising her five children, Deloris focused on their individualism and allowed each of her kids to develop the skills they needed to thrive in life. During an interview with ESPN, Deloris said that she always encouraged her children to find their own special gifts, understand how to use their talents to get the most gains, and follow the path that works for them, not necessarily what others will do.

Their living conditions also resulted in them focusing a lot of time on their children's extracurricular activities. Since Deloris and James both worked full-time to provide for their offspring, they took advantage of their children's involvement in sports to keep them busy and supervised when they had to be at work. Deloris's pragmatic approach to child-rearing, utilizing sports as a tool for development and supervision, reflects a deep understanding of parenting strategies.

Despite towering over many of his opponents on the basketball court and standing six feet six inches tall, there was a time when Michael desperately wished to be taller. During her ESPN interview, Deloris recalled how she would tell him to "go put salt in your shoes and pray" whenever he would moan about not being tall enough. "He would tell me I was being silly, but I had to pacify him so I could finish dinner," she said. They would also tell young Michael that he had it in his heart to be as tall as he wanted to be. All he had to do to believe in himself (and as such, grow taller), was to change the way he thought about himself and his own abilities (Quihuiz, 2023). This was also the inspiration for Deloris's first children's book, *Salt in His Shoes*.

Apart from being known for his height, Michael has also become synonymous with the sports apparel company Nike. However, had it not been for Deloris, this profitable partnership might never have happened. Michael explained that when he was first invited to meet with the bigwigs at Nike, he wasn't interested and, initially, refused to go. Not even his agent could convince him to go, until Deloris stepped in.

Michael explains that his mother gave him no other option but to get onto the plane to go to the meeting with Nike. Once the sports apparel company made their pitch, it was again his parents who told him that he'd be a fool if he didn't take the deal. After signing his first deal with Nike in 1984, his signature sneaker, the now iconic *Air Jordan*, was developed, which included a healthy paycheck for Michael.

He never forgot the role his mother played in securing this partnership and the legacy that followed, and in 2021, Michael honored Deloris by creating another shoe, *Dear Deloris*. Deloris' role in Michael's Nike deal is also the basis for the 2023 film *Air*, directed by Ben Affleck, in which Academy Award-winning actress Viola Davis plays the role of Deloris.

Losing her husband to a senseless murder in 1993 was tough on Deloris, but she remained strong for her five children. Michael talks openly about how his whole family supported each other during this difficult time but it was his mother in particular who helped him work through his grief. She reminded him that even though their situation seemed very negative, there was always something positive to find and be grateful for. Michael says that his dad always taught him the benefit of turning any negative into a positive. After his father's death, Michael decided to make this advice a mantra that he still lives by.

Despite achieving huge success in his sport, Michael remembered the values Deloris taught him, which included cleaning his own house. Since his mother made sure her children did their chores in the family home, he got so used to doing this around the house and cleaning up after himself, that fame and fortune couldn't change him. Deloris says learning and doing these life skills—which included dusting, cooking, and hemming his pants—were "a result of such parental expectations" (Fleming, 2023).

In her parenting book, *Family First: Winning the Parenting Game*, Deloris talks about her trials and tribulations in raising her five children. She explained that her four pillars of parenthood are perseverance, faith, integrity, and having a strong identity. She also admits that in disciplining her five children, she went against what is commonly believed to be inappropriate punishment by "physically punishing" all five of her children.

In her powerful book, Deloris shows her vulnerability and never claims to be the perfect mother of having had well-mannered children. Instead, she openly discusses some of the challenges she experienced, such as the time when Michael was suspended from school at the age of 13. Since Deloris and James both worked full-time, Michael had no choice but to tag along with her to work. She parked her car close to the window so she could keep an eye on it throughout the day, and left Michael in the car to study while she was working. That was the last time he was ever suspended (Fleming, 2023).

The Ripple Effect of Deloris' Influence on Michael Jordan's Success

Michael Jordan's impact transcends the world of basketball. He's a shining example of inspiration and mentorship across various fields. His journey and principles have profoundly influenced peers, emerging athletes, and even entrepreneurs.

Players like Kobe Bryant and LeBron James have openly acknowledged Michael as a significant role model. Kobe often referred to Michael as his "big brother," emulating his work ethic and competitive spirit. In a heartfelt tribute, Kobe once shared how Michael's mentorship extended beyond the court, offering advice on handling pressure and staying focused. LeBron, the basketball superstar who Michael narrowly edged out as the greatest player in NBA history according to The Athletic's poll of 133 players, has frequently highlighted Michael's influence on his career. In an interview, LeBron explained, "I wanted to be like MJ. I wanted to shoot fadeaways like MJ. I wanted to stick out my tongue on dunks like MJ, wear my sneakers like MJ. I wanted kids to look up at me someday like MJ" (Medina, 2019).

But Michael's impact reaches far beyond the court, as he dedicates himself to meaningful community contributions and philanthropic work. In many respects, it's a continuation of the voluntary work in the community that his parents encouraged him to do in his youth, but now on a much larger scale thanks to his global reach as arguably the most recognizable sports star ever.

One of the most significant initiatives under his name is the Jordan Brands Wings program. This program is dedicated to providing educational opportunities to underprivileged youth, aiming to empower them through scholarships, mentorship, and various educational resources. "My mother and my teachers inspired the creation of the Wings program by placing a high value on education and passing that on to me," Michael was quoted as saying in an interview when asked to comment on the driving force behind the creation of his program (Kher, 2024).

Recognizing the barriers that this vulnerable group often face, the program focuses on creating pathways to success through financial support and educational initiatives. By offering scholarships to high-achieving students from low-income backgrounds, the program ensures that financial constraints do not hinder their academic aspirations. These scholarships cover tuition and related educational expenses, alleviating the burden on students and their families.

Beyond financial support, the Wings program emphasizes the importance of mentorship. Partnering with educational institutions and community organizations, the program connects students with mentors who provide guidance, support, and encouragement. These mentors, often professionals and educators, help students navigate their academic and personal challenges, fostering a supportive environment for growth.

The Wings program also extends its reach through various community engagement initiatives. By organizing workshops, seminars, and extracurricular activities, the program encourages students to develop their skills and interests.

The impact of the Wings program can be seen in the success stories of its beneficiaries. Many scholarship recipients have gone on to attend prestigious universities and pursue successful careers, attributing their achievements to the support they received from the program. These success stories serve as a testament to the program's effectiveness and its role in transforming lives.

Michael Jordan's vision for the Wings program reflects his belief in the power of education as a tool for social change—a belief handed down from Deloris. And it's through initiatives like Wings that Michael continues to demonstrate the values of giving back that Deloris instilled in him, namely that true greatness extends beyond personal achievements to include uplifting and empowering others.

Inspiration Lingers Long After the Final Buzzer

Michael Jordan is so much more than jaw-dropping dunks, numerous trophies, and highlight reels. He's more thanks to his mother, Deloris. Her story, along with those of other sports moms, shows just how important mothers are in shaping the lives and careers of athletes. In fact, professional athletes frequently acknowledge their mothers' impact on their successes in and out of the arena.

One of the most heartwarming examples is Kevin Durant's shout-out to his mother, Wanda, during his 2014 NBA MVP speech. He called her the "real MVP" and spoke about her sacrifices and endless support in helping him reach the top of the NBA. The speech connected with a lot of people and brought Wanda into the spotlight, making her a celebrity of sorts. To this day she's regularly booked for speaking engagements where she talks about how she raised her sons and offers parenting tips and strategies. But even before the infamous speech, Wanda was looking to help others in a meaningful way. In 2013, she spearheaded the establishment of the Durant Family Foundation (DFF), which runs educational, athletic, and social programs to help at-risk youth from low-income backgrounds.

Similarly, NFL star Roddy White credited his mother, Joenethia, for giving him the tough love and guidance he needed to succeed. If it wasn't for her toughness in convincing the local recreation department and then the team coach to let her young son play despite his shorter than average stature, who knows if Roddy would've even played football at any level. From his days in high school, college, and the NFL, Roddy has been setting records like a man possessed. He says he always plays with the same passion and dogged determination to do his best that Joenethia showed when fighting for his place on the local team. And their impact doesn't stop there. The Roddy White Keep the Faith Foundation (RWKTFF) empowers youth to reach their potential, with Joenethia unsurprisingly running things as the Principal Officer.

Olympic gold medalist Simone Biles has openly acknowledged the pivotal role her adoptive parents have played in her life and career. It was Simone's biological grandfather and his wife who adopted her and her younger sister Adria at age six. Soon after, they enrolled her in her very first gymnastics classes and she instantly impressed the coaches with her abilities and attitude. Her mother Nellie has always made it a priority to attend any event Simone participates in. She believes that being there in person, despite how nerve wracking she finds it, gives her daughter the confidence to perform to the best of her ability knowing that she has the love and support of her family no matter what the result. Simone gives back to the community by working with the Friends of the Children program, hoping to make a difference in the lives of children in foster care.

These are just three examples of top class athletes who, like Michael, have a lot of appreciation for the efforts of their mothers. The broader impact of mothers on athletes' careers was also recognized in the global "Thank You, Mom" campaign by P&G during the 2010 Olympics.

The campaign showcased the heartwarming and often overlooked role of mothers in nurturing and supporting future athletes. By sharing real-life stories of mothers who juggled countless responsibilities to help their kids chase Olympic dreams, P&G struck a deep emotional chord with viewers. The ads celebrated everyday moments like driving to early morning practices and providing comforting words after tough games, painting a vivid picture of the sacrifices and love that go into raising a champion. This campaign tugged at heartstrings while honoring the unsung heroes who are crucial to many athlete's journey to the top.

And the experts agree. When parents are actively involved in their children's education and extracurricular activities, including sports, it significantly contributes to their achievement, self-regulation, and motivation (Eccles & Harold, 1993). This involvement ranges from logistical support, like taking them to practices and watching their games, to emotional support, including encouragement and validation of effort and perseverance.

We can clearly see this involvement in the stories in this chapter. In Michael's case, Deloris made sure that her children always had someone from the family attending their games, if not the parents themselves, then a sibling would go, even if they'd recently fallen out. In the words of Nellie Biles, "The important thing is to be there for Simone and making sure that she understands that her family is there giving her her full support" (Caplan, 2024). This continuous love and support from an early age instilled important values in each of the athletes and inspired them to take advantage of their status and success to give back to causes close to their hearts.

The real win then, as the mothers of these famous athletes show us, isn't just about what you achieve for yourself or your children. It's about inspiring others, making a positive impact in your community, and leaving something behind that lasts longer than any sports record.

Chapter 5:

Esther Wojcicki

Parents need to stop coddling their kids. The more you trust your children to do things on their own, the more empowered they'll be.

Esther Wojcicki

Empowering Independence

For nine years, she was the CEO of the biggest online video-sharing platform in the world while also being a wife and mother of five. To say Susan Wojcicki perfected the art of keeping her private and professional lives separate would be a massive understatement. Susan blocked off specific hours every night to spend with her family without answering any important work emails or calls. She was even able to successfully work with her former brother-in-law for years after her sister's divorce.

Susan studied history and literature at Harvard University. While she was initially interested in journalism, her view of the world changed when she took an introductory computer science course. She finished her master's degree in economics from the University of California before taking up her first job in the marketing department at the computer company Intel.

Her big break came when Susan and her husband, Dennis Troper, rented out their garage for extra income to help make ends meet. Their tenants were two doctoral students, Larry Page and Sergey Brin, with the latter marrying Susan's sister Anne and staying together for eight years. It was in Susan's garage that Larry and Sergey invented the search engine company Google. Susan fondly remembers how they would spend late nights together in the garage eating pizza and M&Ms, dreaming about the impact Google could make on the world. A year after Google went live, Susan joined as its 16th employee, heading their marketing department. Her first task was to incorporate holidays and other special events into the company's logo on the search page, enhancing the visual appeal and making it more engaging for users.

After this, she helped monetize Google by creating AdSense, took charge of Google Videos, their free video-sharing platform, and eventually convinced Larry and Sergey to buy their biggest competitor, YouTube, which she headed as CEO for nine years before stepping down in 2023.

When you look at Susan's life to understand her vast success and what sets her apart from other CEOs around the world, your attention immediately goes to her mother, a powerhouse herself, Esther Wojcicki.

Esther Wojcicki's Journey and Influence

Esther, fondly known as Woj by many, is a fantastic role model on how to juggle family and work life: Not only is she a mother of three daughters—who all became highly successful in their own rights: two became CEOs of international companies with the third a doctor researching HIV and obesity in children—but also had a highly successful career as an educator and journalist. It comes as no surprise that she also became a best-selling author when she published the book, *How to Raise Successful People: Simple Lessons for Radical Results* in 2019.

Judging by the successes her three daughters have enjoyed in life, Esther clearly had amazing triumphs in her journey through motherhood. However, she never claimed to know all the answers, as she recalls, "I used [my children] as guinea pigs. I tried all my education philosophy on them" (Coudriet, 2019).

Growing up, Esther experienced many hardships. Born in 1941 as the daughter of immigrants from Russia and Ukraine living in New York, Esther grew up in an impoverished environment. She didn't want that for her future and realized the only way out was to get an education. When she was only 10 years old, she decided that she would study as much as she could with the hopes of giving her future family the best life possible. After leaving school, she first qualified as a journalist and then as a teacher. She chose the latter career as she enjoyed being surrounded by other people and had a deep desire to help others turn into the best versions of themselves.

Esther's parenting journey was made easy by Susan, a model child and hard worker who barely showed any signs of the rebellious nature many teenagers adopt. "She was boring like that," recalls Esther jokingly. The most rebellious act Susan ever did was to go to India as a photographer after completing her Harvard degree (Luscombe, 2015).

Trust, Freedom, and Encouraging Autonomy

Esther has always been vocal about her opinions, particularly when it comes to her daughters and their well-being. Susan remembers how her mother made official complaints about the quality of education at her daughters' school, which taught Susan the importance of standing up for yourself and what you believe is right. As she got more involved in improving the quality that she felt was sorely lacking, Esther developed a journalism program. This sparked Susan's interest and led to her becoming active in her school newspaper. Esther also encouraged her eldest daughter to develop her keen sense for business: Susan was only 11 years old when she sold spice ropes, which are basically plaited yarn threaded with spices, in her neighborhood.

In the same way that Esther is outspoken about her well-behaved eldest daughter, she openly speaks and writes about her parenting style and agrees that how she chose to raise her children may go against what many others would believe is right or ideal. Her number-one parenting rule is you should never do something for your child that they can do on their own. She also believes that parents should stop removing every obstacle their children might face. Instead, they need to gain real-world experience and fail so that they can learn and grow.

Instead of making life easier for her children, she developed her now famous method, "I do, we do, you do" (Harder, 2022). She first showed her children how to do something, then she did it with them, and after that, she left them to do things on their own. She also advocates the importance of showing her children that she trusts them. Esther believes that trusting your children to make decisions by themselves will empower them to feel more confident and engaged in their own lives. Once they reach this level of empowerment, the sky is the limit for what they can achieve.

During an interview Susan did with Esther as part of the *Huffington Post*'s parenting series #TalkToMe, Susan mentioned the success both she and her sisters acquired in their careers, and jokingly asked Esther what she gave them for breakfast. To this, Esther replied that she focused on giving her daughters freedom in all the choices they had to make, even what they ate that morning. However, once they made a decision or a choice, her children had to live with it, even if it wasn't a good decision. She didn't help her daughters overcome the challenges caused by their own decisions. As an example, Esther spoke about a hot pink rug that Susan chose for her room when she was around five years old. Even though Esther didn't like the rug at all, she allowed her daughter to keep it for 10 years. She believes this is where many modern parents make mistakes: They don't give their children the necessary independence or continuously worry that if they don't control every aspect of their children's lives, they won't be successful as adults.

The freedom that Esther gave her daughters is directly opposite to helicopter parenting that is often practiced, where parents accept responsibility for their children's actions and place high focus on doing whatever they can to help their children reach success. Esther believes helicopter parenting creates an environment where children grow into adults with poor self-confidence and coping skills, along with high levels of anxiety and entitlement.

To avoid this, Esther developed her TRICK acronym for parenting, as she wrote in her book:

- **Trust**: Parents need to show their children that they trust them. Once they experience this level of trust, they will feel empowered.
- **Respect**: Parents should respect their children, their choices, and what they choose their lives to look like.
- **Independence**: If there is a strong foundation of trust and respect, children will become independent, which will help them cope with setbacks and boredom.
- **Collaboration**: Parents should work with their children rather than against them in all things, including making decisions and discipline.

- **Kindness**: If parents can model gratitude and forgiveness, their children will become more aware of what's going on in the world around them.

Esther's TRICK framework was a practical guide that she applied consistently while raising her three daughters. She made sure they had everything they needed but not necessarily everything they wanted. She believes this played a major role in her daughters' success, as they would have to think of ways they could get what they wanted by themselves. "If you think about how to get creativity and innovation, it comes when you don't have everything," Esther said at a Forbes Women's Summit in 2019 (Coudriet, 2019).

This is something Susan also practiced when she was raising her five children. Despite being the big boss of YouTube, she set screen time limits to help them stay in the present, including restrictions on watching YouTube. On some vacations, she would even take their phones away completely.

In Susan's interview with her mother, she refers to Esther's silly side, and asks her why she was so crazy. To this, Esther answers that when you face challenges, you can either cry about it or find the humor in the situation. "It's important to enjoy life" (HuffPost, 2016).

The Ripple Effect of Esther's Influence on Susan Wojcicki's Success

Esther Wojcicki is a pioneering mother and educator whose influence on her daughters, the children that she teaches, her peers, and other mothers around the world cannot be overstated. Susan's passionate advocacy for women in tech can be traced back to her upbringing, allowing Esther's guidance to reach a whole new group of people.

Susan has always been vocal about the challenges women face in the tech industry. She's emphasized the need for more female role models and leaders, which is crucial in a field where women are often underrepresented. She's written essays and given speeches on the importance of gender equality in tech, including her response to gender bias controversies. By following Esther's example and speaking out for something she believes in, she's helping to draw attention to the issue and inspire change.

Under Susan's leadership, YouTube saw significant strides in gender diversity. She increased the percentage of female employees from 24% to 30%. This might seem like a small number, but in the tech world, it's a big deal. Her commitment to gender diversity goes beyond simply hiring more women. Thanks to Susan, YouTube launched programs specifically aimed at supporting and promoting female content creators. Initiatives like YouTube Spaces provide resources and opportunities for creators to collaborate and grow their channels. This support is vital for encouraging more women to step into the spotlight and share their voices.

Susan's experience as a mother has influenced her to champion parental support policies at Google and YouTube. In fact, she was four months pregnant when she first joined Google and the first at the company to go on maternity leave. She introduced 18 weeks of paid maternity leave, setting a standard for the tech industry. Esther often spoke about the importance of balancing work and family, which is something Susan integrated into her own professional life, who then created an environment where other mothers had a chance to do the same. The valuable workplace benefit cut the rate of new mothers leaving the company by a massive 50%. In case you're wondering, new fathers get 12 weeks paid paternity leave, bringing additional relief to new parents navigating the challenges of working in the tech industry and raising a newborn.

Like her mother, Susan is also passionate about education. She has partnered with educational organizations to promote STEM (Science,

Technology, Engineering, and Mathematics) education among young women and girls. These partnerships aim to inspire the next generation of female tech leaders and close the gender gap in these fields. But talking is only the first step in Esther's "I do, we do, you do" mantra, and so Susan is well aware of the importance of mentorship in fostering independence. That's why she's actively involved in mentorship programs and initiatives that provide support and guidance to women in tech. Her involvement helps to create a network of support, empowering more women to enter and succeed in the industry.

The ripple effect of Esther Wojcicki is a narrative about the power of intergenerational influence and the enduring impact of strong female leadership that extends beyond her immediate family. Susan's work continues to inspire and motivate, showing the world that women can lead, innovate, and excel in technology.

When Motherhood Is Just a Simple Trick

When trying to find other examples like Esther Wojcicki, it was impossible to find another mother who quite measured up to her unique influence. After all, she literally wrote the book on how to raise successful people. Her approach, summed up in her somewhat contradictory-sounding TRICK framework shaped the remarkable careers of not one, but all three of her daughters; Susan, Janet, and Anne. They don't call her the godmother of Silicon Valley for nothing, you know!

Any parent looking to specifically guide their children towards success in the burgeoning tech industry can draw significant inspiration from Esther Wojcicki's parenting approach. Anne Wojcicki, co-founder and CEO of the personal genomics company 23andMe, also thrived under the same nurturing framework. Anne's work in making genetic testing accessible to the public has revolutionized the way people understand their health. Esther's principles of trust and independence were evident as Anne navigated the complex world of biotech startups, making bold decisions that led to the success of 23andMe. The respect Esther showed for Anne's scientific interests and the collaborative environment she fostered at home enabled Anne to build a company that succeeded commercially while making a significant societal impact.

Esther's unwavering **Trust** in her daughter's capabilities allowed them to pursue their interests freely. From a young age, they were trusted to make their own decisions, whether it was about their education or their burgeoning interests in technology and science. This trust empowered them to take risks and explore their fields. For Susan, this meant venturing into the world of computer science, leading to her pivotal role at Google. Anne, on the other hand, delved into genetics, co-founding a revolutionary genomics company.

Esther showed **Respect** for her children's individual interests and ambitions, never pushing them into predefined roles but rather encouraging them to follow their passions. Susan's initial interest in history and literature was met with the same respect as her later shift to economics and computer science. This respect for her choices cultivated a sense of self-worth and confidence in Susan, essential traits for any leader in the competitive tech industry.

Esther's encouragement of **Independence** was another cornerstone of her parenting. She allowed her girls to learn through experience, making their own decisions and learning from both successes and failures, even if it meant going to school on an empty stomach after preparing themselves a less-than-appetizing breakfast.

Esther instilled the value of teamwork and cooperation, essential qualities in the tech world where **Collaboration** often leads to groundbreaking innovations. Just look at Susan's ability to work effectively within Google's dynamic team, her leadership in developing AdSense, and her role in acquiring YouTube as evidence. Anne, too, benefited from this collaborative mindset, as she built a team at 23andMe that combined expertise from various disciplines to create a product that is both scientifically robust and consumer-friendly.

Esther modeled **Kindness**, teaching her children to consider the broader impact of their work on society. This principle guided Susan's leadership style, where she emphasized ethical considerations and social responsibility, especially as an outspoken advocate for women in tech. It wasn't just about technological advancement for Susan; it was about using technology to make a positive difference in the world. Anne also lives this value, as she focuses on empowering individuals with information about their genetic makeup, thereby promoting personal health and well-being.

Esther Wojcicki proves that the right guidance can indeed create technology leaders who are equipped to make a lasting, positive impact on the world. And there's no "trick" to it really. Just give your children trust, respect, independence, collaboration, and kindness, and watch them grow into pioneers who shape the future of technology and society.

Chapter 6:

Jackie Bezos

I won the lottery with my mom. Thanks for literally everything, Mom.

Jeff Bezos

The Architect of Innovation

To be innovative means you create something new that brings about positive change, either to the world or people's lives. Jeff Bezos perfected the art of innovation when he created Amazon.

Jeff was born in New Mexico to a teenage mother and a young, alcoholic father. When he was only four, his mother remarried, and his new stepfather adopted him. As you'll soon discover, little Jeff was an atypical toddler, often tinkering with tech rather than playing with toys.. But it was when he was still in high school that he tasted his first real success of a long career in innovation when he created the Dream Institute, a center that promoted creativity in young students. After high school, he obtained degrees in electrical engineering and computer science from Princeton University. And after college, he worked at D.E. Shaw & Co, an investment bank based in New York, where he later became their youngest senior vice president. While at the bank, Jeff was tasked with investigating online investment opportunities. This was how his idea of opening an online bookstore was developed.

In 1994, Jeff quit his job at the bank, moved to Seattle, and appointed a handful of employees to help him develop the software that would later become Amazon. This ground-breaking work was done from the garage of Jeff's rented home. A year later, the first book was sold on Amazon, named after the South American river, with the site quickly branching out to include other products and eventually becoming the worldwide leader in e-commerce.

Had it not been for the encouragement from his mother, Jackie, who together with Jeff's adopted father became the first investors in Amazon, he might never have been brave enough to quit his corporate job to focus on innovation. But of course, the story of Amazon's mammoth success started decades earlier and at the hands of one stellar woman.

Jackie Bezos' Journey and Influence

Born in 1946 in New Mexico, Jacklyn "Jackie" Gise was raised by a loving and supportive family. In high school, she met Jeff's biological father, Ted Jorgensen, an avid unicycle hockey player and circus performer. When she was only 16 years old, she fell pregnant with her first child. As was expected of her as a young women, Jackie married Ted and gave birth to Jeff shortly after her 17th birthday. However, when Jeff was just 17 months old, Jackie left Ted to protect her young son from his father's alcoholism.

Jackie and Jeff moved back to her parent's house, and she started working on her first goal: completing her education. The high school she attended before becoming pregnant wanted to block her from completing school. Jackie didn't accept this, as it made no sense that she should be deprived of an education just because she got pregnant. Eventually, the school agreed to allow her back to school, as long as she followed some very specific conditions. Perhaps the harshest of which being that she couldn't socialize with any of the other students.

After finishing school, Jackie took secretarial classes, which allowed her to get her first job as a secretary. "Even though I was a terrible typist and couldn't read my own shorthand, somebody actually hired me," Jackie said during an interview (Clifford, 2019). She didn't earn a big salary but was able to get an apartment for herself and baby Jeff. After paying the rent and buying food, Jackie had no money left for any luxuries, which included having a phone. Her parents insisted on having daily contact with their daughter and grandson, so they gave her a walkie-talkie. Because she didn't have to worry about paying a phone bill, they were able to afford to stay in their apartment. What makes Jackie's story even more amazing is that she didn't come from a poor family. But rather than live off the financial support of her father, she chose to prove to the world that she had the ability and the bravery to go it alone.

Jackie later married Mike Bezos, a refugee from Cuba, who adopted four-year-old Jeff. They also had two children together, a daughter named Christina and a son called Mark. The Bezos family continued to thrive in later decades and through the Bezos Family Foundation. The Foundation is dedicated to creating learning opportunities for children as well as adults, giving Jackie the opportunity to give back to others who find themselves in a similar position to the one she was in when she ventured out on her own with little Jeff in tow.

Igniting Curiosity and Embracing Innovation

Even though many would argue that Jackie was still a child herself when Jeff was born, she knew from the start that her son was special. This was evident when she took him to an amusement park when he was only about two-and-a-half years old. While all the other children were excited about the different rides, little Jeff was only interested in how the motors and machines of those rides worked. At home, instead of playing with his toys, he tried to take his crib apart using a screwdriver. Jackie said that it was during those times she knew he wasn't just wired differently but that he was destined for greatness.

Jackie wanted to provide her son with the best possible life, so she enrolled in night school to further her education. Unfortunately, this left her with the problem of what to do with Jeff while she was at school, as she didn't have enough money to pay a babysitter. After pleading her case with her professors, some allowed her to bring her baby with her to school, so she picked her classes based on who would allow Jeff to attend with her. She went to class with her infant in one arm and two duffel bags in the other. One of these bags was filled with diapers, bottles, and textbooks, while the other bag was filled with toys to keep little Jeff preoccupied while she tried to focus on her lectures.

It was at these night classes that she met Mike, who bonded with Jeff instantly. Miguel "Mike" Bezos fled to America from his homeland of Cuba at just 16 years old and without knowing any English. It's a testament to his courage and hardworking nature that he would go on to further his education and later secure a prestigious position at Exxon, where he eventually had the means to invest in his dear son's risky endeavor.

Jackie later enrolled at Saint Elizabeth College, where she graduated at the age of 40. "Finally, after delays and setbacks, I feasted at the table of higher education. And boy did I feast. I was relentless. I devoured my classes," Jackie said. She is open about this being the proudest she has ever been of herself (Clifford, 2019).

Her incredible will to want to make the best of her life and do whatever it takes to get there inspired Mike to look differently at his own life and the challenges he faced. Whenever he couldn't find a way to overcome a problem or difficult situation, he followed her example and used his imagination to create innovative solutions.

Jackie's eagerness to learn, despite being well beyond the typical age of a college student, meant that Jeff grew up with an amazing role model of a mother who read, which nurtured his own love for books. When he wanted to create his online book store, Jackie and Mike didn't just provide emotional support but financial support as well. During the start-up of his company, Jeff convinced 22 people to invest in his company, with two of them being Jackie and Mike. They offered an investment of nearly $250,000, securing them a 6% share in Amazon.

Jeff explained that he warned them of the risk of losing all their money. After all, if the gamble didn't work out and they ended up losing all their money, he still wanted to be able to go home for Thanksgiving, he joked. However, Jeff's parents admitted that they didn't quite understand the business Jeff wanted to create, but they had complete faith in their son. They knew that with enough encouragement and support, Jeff was destined for greatness.

Jeff admitted that the support he received from his parents throughout his life inspired him to take the necessary risks to reach his goals. "When you have loving and supportive people in your life... you end up being able to take risks" (Eidell, 2023).

If it wasn't for the strong values Jackie instilled in her three children, Jeff's life could've looked completely different, especially when he discovered at the age of ten that Mike wasn't his biological father. However, despite knowing the truth, Jeff never once had a desire to meet Ted and continued to regard Mike as his father.

He also shares a tight bond with his half-sister Christina and half-brother Mark. This bond is due to the caring and nurturing role Jackie played in all their lives. She worked hard to make sure all her children stayed close and had each other's backs no matter what happened. "I won that lottery of having so many people in my life who have given me that unconditional love," Jeff said (Eidell, 2023). Incidentally, Christina and Mark were also early investors in Amazon.

When reading Jackie's story, her love for her family and determination to succeed is evident. In a tribute to Jackie on his X page, Jeff wrote that he still cannot fathom how she was able to do what she did and kept them all safe no matter how bleak their circumstances appeared to be. He makes it clear that he is forever grateful for the sacrifices she made for her family and for sharing her incredible strength with them.

The Ripple Effect of Jackie's Influence on Jeff Bezos' Success

The Bezos Family Foundation (BFF) was founded in 2000 as a family affair, with Jackie and Mike co-founding it along with their three children and their spouses, all of whom serve or served as board members.

The BFF operates four primary programs aimed at supporting learning and development from early childhood through adolescence. The Bezos Scholars Program selects high school students for leadership training and social activism projects. Students Rebuild encourages youth engagement in global causes through art-based challenges. Vroom provides tools for parents to integrate learning into daily routines. Mind in the Making offers training for teaching children life skills and executive functions. These programs, along with the Foundation's grants, champion the science of learning and its application in everyday life—a mission very close to Jackie's heart. The Foundation's approach combines grant-making with in-house programs to spark joyful discovery and learning in young people.

This commitment to education and youth development laid the groundwork for a broader charitable legacy within the Bezos family. While Jeff was not directly involved in founding the BFF, it seems to have influenced his own charitable endeavors, including the Day One Fund and the Bezos Earth Fund.

The Day One Fund focuses on helping homeless families and creating preschools in low-income communities. Just think, were it not for the walkie-talkie Jackie used to keep in touch with her parents and saving the expense of using a phone, she and Jeff could've been living on the streets, or at least struggling to stay in their rental. The Fund awards organizations with the means to further their efforts in helping families get off the streets or out of shelters and into stable housing. The Fund's second area of focus is driven by the same principles that propelled Amazon to success, namely creating environments where learning, invention, and continuous improvement thrive. And where better to create these hubs of inspiration than in childhood education. Like Jackie, Jeff values the role education plays in future success and offers children the chance to thrive in free, full-day, creative learning.

Jeff founded the Bezos Earth Fund with a $10 billion commitment to address climate change and protect nature. The fund aims to support projects that can create systems-level change and foster a just transition to a low-carbon economy. This fund is involved in numerous initiatives around the world, asking everyone everywhere to join the collective effort to create a healthy environment. Where the fund differs, however, is in how we see Jeff's passion for science and technology shining through. The AI for Climate and Nature Grand Challenge offers huge grants to anyone using the same critical thinking skills that he learned from his pioneering work on Amazon to create innovative solutions that leverage big data and artificial intelligence to solve environmental issues like monitoring greenhouse gas emissions and detecting forest fires.

In addition to these major initiatives, Jeff has made other significant charitable contributions. For instance, he awarded $50 million to Eva Longoria, Dolly Parton, and other well-known individuals to give away to various nonprofit groups as they see fit as part of his Courage and Civility Award. His commitment to giving away most of his $124 billion net worth has positioned him as one of the latest mega-philanthropists alongside people like Bill Gates, Elon Musk, and Mark Zuckerberg.

While we can't make a direct connection between the BFF and Jeff's personal philanthropy from any available interview transcripts, it's reasonable to infer that growing up with a mother that valued charitable giving and education likely influenced Jeff's own approach to philanthropy. The foundation established by his parents in 2000 seems to have set a precedent for using wealth to make a positive impact on society, a principle that Jeff has embraced on a much larger scale in recent years.

Listening to Children Is a Skill

From the beginning, Jackie recognized that Jeff was wired a little differently from other kids. Instead of seeing this as a challenge or a reason to visit a specialist, she embraced her son's natural qualities and nurtured his intellectual curiosity.

Jeff had inventive ideas throughout his childhood and adolescence. Jackie gave him the encouragement whenever he needed it, although there were times when it wasn't easy to understand what he was proposing, as was the case later when he suggested a new e-commerce platform called Amazon. And there were times when Jackie would suggest ideas to Jeff for him to develop, like when she challenged him to memorize offensive plays in American football. But ultimately, she listened to Jeff and never stopped him from exploring his talent along paths that he saw fit to follow.

Much like Jackie Bezos, who recognized her son Jeff's intrinsic curiosity, Michelle Fishburne saw her daughter's inventive spirit from an early age. But while Jackie supported Jeff's youthful experiments, Michelle said "When my daughter, Alexis, started inventing as a young kid, I dismissed her creations as anything important" (Fishburne, 2018). Michelle would later come to realize that no-one holds the monopoly on inventing; any ordinary human, at any age, can solve problems with their mind.

Born Chase Lewis, Alexis came out as transgender at age 11, embracing her true identity with her family's unconditional love and support. Michelle allowed Alexis the freedom to explore her passions without judgment or restraint. One of those passions was dreaming up innovative solutions to problems she encountered. It was after learning the heartbreaking reality of mothers in Somalia during the famine, who had to leave the children they couldn't carry by the side of the road to die, that the idea for the Rescue Travois was born. Lightweight yet durable, the sled-like device can transport children or injured adults over difficult terrain using bamboo poles and a recycled plastic base.

Alexis developed a prototype and applied for a patent. When the bamboo travois won national recognition from the IPOEF, Michelle helped her daughter navigate the publicity and opportunities that followed.

Michelle and Jackie have walked similar paths and came to the same realization—don't scoff at your child's ideas if you don't understand them, but instead listen to them and encourage their creativity. Doing so builds belief in their innate human ability to solve problems, which only become more complex as they get older. And sometimes, as in the cases of Jeff and Alexis, it can even pay dividends later in life, for them, for you, and for the world.

Chapter 7:

Mary Lee Pfeiffer

I've always had the same values. Family for me has always been important. When I shoot, everybody comes.

Tom Cruise

The Navigator of Dreams

From death-defying aerial stunts to heart-stopping secret missions and unforgettable romantic lines, this Hollywood A-lister has mastered the art of the blockbuster. He's taken more than his fair share of criticism over his personal beliefs, but no-one could ever say a bad word against his dedication to his craft, which has spanned several decades and shows no sign of slowing down. As one of the world's most successful actors and producers, Tom Cruise is undoubtedly a source of creativity and inspiration.

Following his breakthrough performances in the 1980s, Tom's career skyrocketed with a series of critically acclaimed and commercially successful films. His role as Maverick in *Top Gun* became iconic, making the film the highest-grossing movie of that year and establishing Tom as a leading man in Hollywood. He earned further acclaim with *Rain Man*, before securing his first Academy Award nomination thanks to his powerful depiction of Vietnam War veteran Ron Kovic in *Born on the Fourth of July*.

Throughout the 90s, Tom continued to dominate the box office and receive award nominations. Transitioning into the 2000s, Tom embraced the action genre, most notably as Ethan Hunt in the *Mission: Impossible* series. Dedicated to performing his own stunts, Tom has earned a reputation for his daring and commitment.

But before he became one of the biggest stars in Hollywood, Tom's life was anything but a fairytale. He grew up in a house with a physically abusive father. He and his family were constantly relocating, which meant starting all over again at a new school each time. At school, he struggled severely with the reading disability, dyslexia. And, after his father left them in such poverty, he had to take on jobs to support his mother and three sisters.

Much like Maverick piloting through the skies to save the day, Tom's mother navigated the challenges of single parenthood with daring finesse, rightfully earning her wings as the original maverick behind the movie star. Because despite his rough start to life, Tom rose to riches and, until the day of her death in 2017, he treated his mother, Mary Lee Pfeiffer, like the queen she was. She was also the major motivator that pushed Tom into acting, as Mary Lee noticed his raw talent from a young age.

Mary Lee Pfeiffer's Journey and Influence

Born in Louisville, Kentucky, in 1936, Mary Lee lived a wholesome life of devotion and giving. She spent her career working as a teacher, specifically helping children with special needs get the most out of education.

Mary Lee married Thomas Cruise Mapother III, an electrical engineer who struggled severely to hold a job, resulting in the family being unable to settle anywhere. They first moved to Syracuse, New York, where Tom, the couple's third child and only son, was born, before moving to Ottawa, Canada.

Her marriage was tumultuous, to say the least. During an interview with *Parade*, Tom spoke of his father who physically abused his young children, calling him a coward and a bully who would do whatever he could to gain his family's trust, just to break this same trust by physically abusing them if anything went wrong. Tom explained that he felt like, "There's something wrong with this guy. Don't trust him. Be careful around him" (Palmeri, 2023).

After taking the brave decision to end her marriage in 1974, Mary Lee and her children returned to the United States. The family often moved around, hoping to create a better life in the next city. This meant that over 14 years, Tom attended 15 different schools. They eventually moved to Glen Ridge, New Jersey, where Mary Lee met Jack South, a World War II veteran. They got married in 1978. Tom recalled that Jack loved Mary Lee so deeply that he was willing to take in and help her raise all of her children. Jack's presence also reduced the burden Tom felt for supporting his family, which meant he could refocus on his dreams of a career in acting.

Mary Lee's involvement with the Church of Scientology began later in her life, significantly influenced by her son, who is one of the most high-profile members of the church. Her involvement remained significant until her passing in 2017, with her memorial service being held at her local Church of Scientology, attended by family, friends, and fellow Scientologists.

Cultivating Passion and Perseverance

As a youngster, Tom was passionate about sports, including baseball and hockey, but he particularly loved wrestling, and hoped to pursue a career in this field. Unfortunately, a knee injury sidelined him from this sport, and he had to find another passion to pursue. Since he absolutely hated going to school, where he would try to hide his dyslexia from his classmates, the likelihood of Tom wanting to continue his education beyond high school was slim.

Growing up, Mary Lee fell in love with theater and acting. Whenever and wherever they settled next, she would seek out a local theatre group. She told *Rolling Stone* that even though she was always interested in performing arts, attempting to make it big in Hollywood was considered too big of a risk.

When her young son needed to find something else that sparked his interest, she immediately drew on her love for the performing arts and encouraged him to participate in a local theater group. After all, he would spend many nights entertaining his mother with his impromptu acting skits in the living room. Since then, his mother had been his biggest supporter.

A major shift came after Tom followed her advice to take part in his high school's production of *Guys and Dolls*. After the play, Tom asked Mary Lee and Jack if he could try his skills in show business for the next 10 years. Without giving it any thought, they both agreed. She told *Rolling Stone,* Tom had a "God-given talent… So, we gave him our blessing—and the rest is history" (Heyman, 2017). Until he got his big break in acting, he waited tables to earn an income.

Tom is known in Hollywood as an extremely hard-working actor with an excellent work ethic. This is another thing he inherited from his mother. Growing up, the family was poor, and Mary Lee worked three jobs to try to make ends meet and feed her four children. Many nights, Tom would massage his mother's sore feet after a long, hard day at work. Eventually, Tom also pitched in to help his mother pay the bills, especially when she developed a herniated disc after the stress of her workload took its toll on her health.

There were also many times when the family had to rely on food stamps to ensure everyone had something to eat. One Christmas, the family's financial situation was so dire that they wrote poems for each other as presents. During an interview with *Playboy*, Tom explained that he started working for money when he was about eight years old. He would cut grass, rake leaves, deliver newspapers, and sell special events cards around the neighborhood, basically whatever he could to earn money to help out at home.

Tom always has immense praise for Mary Lee, resulting in a strong, lifelong bond between mother and son. She taught her son that every person has the ability to create their own life. He saw that she did everything she could to give her children the best possible upbringing. "My mother was the one who rose to the occasion. She said, 'We're going to get through this'" (*Who*, 2020). As you'll read in the next section, Tom has never forgotten Mary Lee's mantra and rose to the occasion himself when the film industry, and pretty much the whole world, shut down for what seemed like eternity in 2020.

Tom is known for doing his own stunts in his movies, with his years of wrestling no doubt providing him with excellent stunt man training. But Mary Lee was quite the risk taker too. The mother-son duo often went on adventures together, which even included Tom treating her to a skydiving experience for Mother's Day in the 1990s. "She wasn't necessarily a daredevil, but she had just a wonderful sense of adventure and she was someone that always the cup was half full," he said (*Who*, 2020).

Mary Lee was often seen on Tom's arm at red-carpet events, always supporting her successful son in the same way he has supported her throughout his life. Her presence at these events symbolizes their shared sense of adventure and positivity in the face of life's challenges and also the reciprocal nature of their bond.

The Ripple Effect of Mary Lee's Influence on Tom Cruise's Success

Tom Cruise is a legend in Hollywood. No one could argue with that. You'd also struggle to convince anyone that he only made it to the top thanks to his dashing good looks. In reality, he approaches acting with the very same unwavering dedication and a formidable work ethic he's shown since he was eight years old working odd jobs around the neighborhood to help his family. And those are the exact values he internalized by watching his mother.

His commitment to filmmaking was vividly illustrated during the recent production of *Top Gun: Maverick*, where co-star Miles Teller was particularly struck by Tom's nonstop effort and ridiculous attention to detail. He thought the level of dedication Tom brought to the project was unparalleled. This intensity and passion for his craft no doubt helped the film become a major box office success, surpassing $1 billion worldwide. Miles thought Tom deserved an Oscar for the extreme effort he put into making the film but probably missed out on a nomination because "he makes it all look easy" (Libbey, 2023).

Jennifer Connelly, who also worked alongside him in *Top Gun: Maverick*, expressed profound admiration for Tom, calling him "just perfect" (Murray, 2023). She was impressed by how much he brought to every moment of the filmmaking process, and it made working with him a privilege.

Tom's relentless positivity and drive has made him a beloved figure among directors, actors, crew members, and industry friends alike. He cares deeply about the people he works with and feels a heavy responsibility for their livelihood like they were part of his family.

An example of Tom's incredible spirit in action was during the recent lockdown when everyone was stuck at home climbing the walls. Remote work was a possibility for many people, but what could those working on set or on location do at home? You see, Tom's movie, *Mission: Impossible 7*, was set to start filming when he got the call to cancel his trip to the shooting location in Italy. The studio had shut the film down.

Tom recognized the difficult financial situation crew members and cinema workers, people who must work closely with colleagues and the public, would find themselves in if his movie was not going to be filmed. So, he took it upon himself to establish the rule book for filming during a pandemic and used his powerful influence to convince governments in each location to accept them. This got everyone back on set, where the entire crew worked according to strict safety protocols.

Some said they would've lost their homes if it wasn't for Tom's intervention. To a larger degree, Tom saved cinema.

Recall how Tom remembers Mary Lee as someone who would rise to the occasion and get everyone through sticky situations. Well, for the benefit of all who work with Tom, or thanks to Tom, her positive attitude in the face of adversity rubbed off on her son, who says he, "always had that ability to just deal with things. My whole life has been like that: 'Okay, what do I do now?'" (Connelly, 2018).

Learning to Stand Up for Yourself

For most people, Tom's legacy is defined by his blockbuster hits and daring stunts. For people he's worked with, he has set new standards in the industry and is admired for his work ethic and professionalism. For those closest to him, Tom's positivity and altruistic actions make him more valuable than the box office success of all his movies combined. No matter which of these groups of people you belong to, you're seeing the result of a journey based in no trivial part upon Mary Lee's influence.

There's another Hollywood action star, whose path to success has been significantly shaped by maternal influence. In fact, the heartthrobs share many similarities, including growing up with a single mother. Incidentally, both men later reconciled with their fathers briefly before their deaths. And while the trauma of not having their fathers around as young boys surely affected them in powerful ways, it was the strength of their mothers that got them to where they are today.

Gerard Butler was born in Paisley, Scotland. At six months old, he and his family moved to Quebec, Canada, but just a year later, his father left his mother, Margaret, to raise him and his two older sisters by herself. She decided to bring the children back to Scotland despite having no money left in her pocket. They stayed with his grandmother in her one-and-a-half-bedroom house until they could get a place of their own. To that end, Margaret studied at a night school, where she actually ended up working at as a teacher and later as a senior lecturer.

Gerard grew up in a working-class neighborhood, where he witnessed his mother's strength firsthand. She stood up to local thugs throwing stones at her windows. She also stood up to the police for the excessive way they reprimanded Gerard for committing the very same offense. He saw his mother as a person who was never afraid to speak her mind to anyone she felt was doing the wrong thing.

Like Tom, Gerard didn't grow up with money. He recalls not feeling poor, however, due to the way his mother carried herself. Margaret always stood by her principles, which has had a lasting impact on Gerard. In particular, she pushed her children to be the best they could be. He said, "I feel like I have a very good work ethic and so much of that comes from my mum" (Ogden, 2016).

While Tom hated high school, Gerard excelled in it. But as he was pursuing a law degree at Glasgow University, he discovered his heart wasn't in it, and like Tom, threw all he had into a new passion: Acting. And we're glad they did because we all get a chance to spend some quality time with these legends from the comfort of our cinema seats.

Chapter 8:

Baria Alamuddin

I think growing up my mother was definitely a role model. She was always a working woman and someone who is independent and cared about her career and cared about being independent but also had balance.

Amal Clooney

Balancing Social Awareness and Personal Ambition

She was born amid a civil war in her country of birth, Lebanon, and after immigrating to England with her family to escape the war, had to teach herself to speak English by watching TV. Still, she didn't let her start in life keep her from achieving success. Now, she's a British barrister and established lawyer who often advises leaders of the United Nations on human rights issues. She also works in the International Court of Justice as well as the International Criminal Tribunal where her expertise and passion have made her a sought-after advisor. Her contributions have had a profound impact on upholding human rights standards all over the world.

While being a legal powerhouse by day, Amal Clooney is also the wife of the Academy Award-winning actor George Clooney, as well as the mother of their twins Ella and Alexander.

Together with her husband, she co-founded the Clooney Foundation for Justice (CFJ). Through this foundation, they have provided crucial support to individuals and communities facing human rights violations, ensuring that their voices are heard and their rights are protected. Amal and George's shared commitment to making a positive impact on the world spans over 40 countries, and its effect has been felt across diverse regions and cultures.

Amal's mother, Baria Alamuddin, provided her with an amazing example of being able to do it all: Raise successful children while having a high-profile career. Baria's illustrious career in journalism spanned decades, during which she interviewed numerous heads of state and tackled pivotal global issues, all while advocating fervently for women's rights in the Middle East. Her unwavering commitment to justice and equality profoundly influenced Amal. As you'll read, Baria's dedication to education and advocacy, coupled with her personal sacrifices and professional achievements, provided Amal with a powerful role model to emulate.

Baria Alamuddin's Journey and Influence

From a young age, Baria was fiercely independent and wouldn't allow others to dictate her life. Born in Lebanon in the late 1940s, her parents got divorced when she was only a year old. She stayed by her mother and considered her the only important person in her life growing up, often copying everything she did. Her mother was a big believer in education and female empowerment and was actually the first Jordanian woman to study at the American University in Beirut, at a time when barely any women in the Middle East were educated.

This period of imitation heavily influenced Baria. Inspired by her mother to follow her dreams, Baria never allowed society to dictate to her or tell her what she couldn't do because of her gender. She had her own set of beliefs, and she made it her life's mission to help others.

Initially, Baria wanted to become a lawyer to help ensure justice was served, but she didn't have the opportunity to study law. Her second-choice career was to study journalism, which gave her the public platform to make a difference. She graduated with a degree in journalism, mass media, and political science from the American University of Beirut in 1972.

After qualifying, Baria started her career in television where she established herself as a political reporter of a Lebanese TV news program. She later moved to print media as an editor and later the editor-in-chief of Media Services Syndicate, a significant position in the media industry.

During her tenure, Baria covered critical global events and interviewed prominent world leaders, such as Margaret Thatcher, Archbishop Makarios of Cyprus, Benazir Bhutto, King Hussain of Jordan, Yasser Arafat, and Fidel Castro, to name a few. Baria was also the last journalist to interview Prime Minister Indira Gandhi. Her legacy in journalism was recognized recently when she received a Lifetime Achievement Award from the 2018 Commonwealth Businesswomen Awards; and the 2018 Arab Women of the Year Award, for Achievement in Media, through Regent's University, London.

She took a short break from her career in 1978 when she was pregnant with, Amal. Baria spent two months in hospital with a serious pregnancy complication, placenta previa, a condition where the placenta attaches low in the uterus. Doctors advised her that it would be safest to abort her baby. However, after Baria saw her daughter's face in a dream, she refused to follow their advice. The decision to defy medical advice and give birth to Amal symbolizes a hope and toughness that would come to define both their lives. After Amal was born, she looked exactly like she did in Baria's dreams.

Baria and her former husband, Ramzi Alamuddin, decided to name their daughter Amal, which means hope. This fitting name choice cleverly portrays a reflection of her mother's emotions during her pregnancy and possibly also an optimism for war-ridden Lebanon.

Baria and Ramzi share another daughter, Tala, and two sons from Ramzi's previous marriage. Like Amal, Tala is an outspoken humanitarian, often giving passionate speeches on the empowerment of women in society. "My dream is that all women are able to live the life they desire, without the boundaries of cultural stereotypes and self-limiting beliefs, and with access to the resources, opportunities and means to embrace confidence and be the very best they can be," Tala shared in a speech at the UN headquarters (Malik, 2023).

Love for Education That Transcended into a Battle for Human Rights

A major part of Amal's desire to invest in herself with the goal of making the world a fairer place comes directly from modeling her mother. In particular, Amal's exposure to her mother's devotion to education and ambition played a major role in her development of excellent academic skills and in her decision to become a successful lawyer. As mentioned, if Baria had had the opportunity, she would've become a lawyer as well. Where Baria uses her journalistic platforms to become a voice for the voiceless, Amal is using her legal expertise to bring basic human rights to people living in inequality.

Baria empowered Amal to think critically and motivated her to challenge norms, pushing her towards carving out her own path in the legal field. The values of social justice and human rights instilled by Baria likely influenced Amal's passion for advocating for marginalized individuals and her dedication to using her legal talents to bring about positive change. Growing up in a supportive family environment characterized by open communication, emotional support, and encouragement gave Amal the confidence and determination to pursue her goals relentlessly.

Despite having a big personality and being very outspoken, Baria never forced her will on any of her children. She understood that her children were unique individuals with their own thoughts, feelings, and desires. And so, she always made sure to respect their decisions and opinions, even when they differed from her own. She has, however, taught her daughter the importance of human rights, transparency, and democracy, and why ensuring that justice is served should always be of the utmost importance. "I didn't influence my children in anything except teaching them the values of life, the morality of life, and I could not be more proud," Baria is quoted as saying (Euronews, 2020).

Amal has echoed this ethos, passionately urging women to stand up for each other and remain united in the fight for each other's rights to create lasting positive change. Drawing strength from her mother's pioneering example, she has built her own extraordinary legacy advocating for human rights on the global stage through her legal work and prestigious appointments.

For instance, Amal was the UK's Special Envoy for Media Freedom where she helped develop recommendations for legal and policy reforms to enhance media freedom. In addition to her legal practice, she has held prominent advisory roles, including Senior Adviser to Kofi Annan, UN Envoy on Syria, and Counsel to the UN Inquiry on the use of armed drones. She has been appointed to various UK government expert panels, such as the Attorney-General's panel on public international law and the Prevention of Sexual Violence in Conflict Initiative. Her advocacy includes representing journalists and political prisoners globally, such as Julian Assange, Khadija Ismayilova, Mohamed Fahmy, and Maria Ressa, as well as Yazidi women seeking justice for genocide by Daesh.

With such an equally impressive list as that of her mother's, Amal Clooney clearly exemplifies the ability to thrive in multiple domains, while being a mother herself mind you, and is ever persistent in her dedication to legal excellence, global advocacy, and contributions to education.

The Ripple Effect of Baria's Influence on Amal Clooney's Success

Amal's passion for women's rights is even more remarkable given that she didn't grow up in such a repressive society like her mother and grandmother, where women were told how they should behave and had less rights than men. It's thanks to the moral foundation instilled by Baria's teachings and first-hand experiences of empathy, that helped Amal become a formidable force. And that's all before she even met her husband and co-founder of the Clooney Foundation for Justice.

In a world where human rights are constantly being violated, the CFJ shines as a symbol of hope. The organization has been a driving force in the global fight for justice and equality since 2016. Their work sounds a lot like the summary of Baria's career; promoting accountability, defending fundamental freedoms, and amplifying the voices of the voiceless.

The Foundation's mission is built on the belief that everyone deserves to live with dignity, free from oppression and persecution. Through legal advocacy, policy initiatives, and strategic partnerships with the likes of the Obama Foundation and the Gates Foundation, the CFJ tackles some of the world's most pressing human rights issues, making a significant impact on countless lives.

The CFJ also influences international human rights policy through partnerships with organizations like the United Nations and the International Criminal Court. Their TrialWatch program monitors criminal trials globally to ensure vulnerable defendants including women and girls receive due process and fair treatment, and ultimately avoid or get out of prison. In a similar initiative, Waging Justice for Women, the CFJ fights to change laws in several countries to better protect women from gender-based discrimination.

In Amal's words, "We can combat the injustice that women face by ensuring that unfair laws are overturned and that those who abuse women are held to account" (Solutions, 2023).

Amal and George use their platform to inspire a new generation of activists. They encourage others to stand up for justice and use their resources to create a more equitable world, carrying the torch of her mother's legacy.

In Her Mother's Shoes

It's a rite of passage for every young girl to try on her mom's shoes and feel what it's like to be her. Whether she did it too or not*, Amal has essentially walked in Baria's footsteps when she became an individual who uses her intelligence and determination to fight for the rights of others.

Just as Baria unwavering advocacy for human rights and tireless career in journalism paved the way for Amal's extraordinary achievements, there's another mother whose pioneering spirit and relentless pursuit of justice laid the foundation for her daughter's remarkable career.

Few names carry the same weight and reverence as Ruth Bader Ginsburg. The late Supreme Court Justice, affectionately known as the "Notorious RBG," was a titan of the legal profession, a trailblazer for gender equality, and an unwavering champion of justice. She left an indelible mark on the American legal landscape and inspired generations of aspiring lawyers.

Ruth was born Joan Ruth Bader to Jewish parents Celia and Nathan Bader in 1933 in Brooklyn, New York. With so many girls in her class named Joan, the teacher started calling her Ruth after taking the advice of Celia, and the name stuck. Like Celia, Ruth faced gender discrimination from an early age. But she made sure the most valuable part of her daughter's journey would not be blocked as hers was: In education. Celia spent time educating her daughter and took her to the library at every opportunity. In time, and through her mother's guidance, Ruth learned to never let societal norms dictate her path.

She went on to graduate from Cornell University in 1954, got married to her Cornell boyfriend Martin "Marty" Ginsburg a month later, and gave birth to daughter Jane in 1955. Then in 1956, she enrolled at Harvard Law School, where she sat top of the class while juggling her studies, motherhood, a husband sick with testicular cancer, and keeping him up with his studies. At Harvard, she was one of only nine women in a class of over 500 students. It was a hostile environment where women were scorned for taking a man's place, but it didn't stop her from excelling. When Martin recovered and got a job in New York after his graduation from Harvard, she transferred to Columbia Law School to complete her final year, and graduated as joint first in her class in 1959.

Despite being an exceptionally talented student, Ruth struggled to find an employer willing to hire a woman. When she did eventually get offers from law firms, the salary offered was a lot less than her male counterparts. Frustrated, Ruth decided to spend time researching in Sweden, where she became deeply inspired by the Swedish culture and by their more equal society. She returned to America and accepted a position as professor at Rutgers University Law School in 1963. Fearing more scorn from authority figures and losing her job, she wore baggy clothes to keep her pregnancy a secret. She kept her job until 1972 when she transferred to Columbia and became the first female professor there to earn tenure.

During the 1970s, Ginsburg led the Women's Rights Project at the American Civil Liberties Union, spearheading efforts against gender discrimination and successfully arguing six landmark cases before the U.S. Supreme Court. In 1980, she was appointed by President Jimmy Carter to the U.S. Court of Appeals for the District of Columbia, where she served for thirteen years until her nomination to the Supreme Court by President Bill Clinton in 1993. She was the second woman to serve on the Supreme Court and worked on important cases right up to her death in 2020 at age 87. As if that wasn't impressive enough, she continued her work and scheduled public appearances despite having multiple cancer diagnoses and undergoing painful treatments and surgeries, showing just how much grit and strength this woman had.

Ruth Bader Ginsburg's journey to the Supreme Court was paved with unfortunate obstacles and shameful discrimination. But her experiences only added fuel to the fire burning inside her to fight for lasting change. In her life and career, she played a major role in changing laws in favor of gender equality, including rights to equal pay, rights to equal education opportunities, and the prohibition of employers discriminating against pregnant employees. She even demanded that the principal of her son's school overcome his gender bias when calling her all the time to discuss her son's misbehavior, telling him, "This child has two parents. Please alternate calls" (Totenberg, 2020b).

RBG has earned her status as a champion of women's rights. But her legacy is intertwined with that of her daughter, Jane, a formidable legal scholar and intellectual property law expert in her own right.

It was during Ruth's time at Columbia that Jane first witnessed her mother's tireless dedication to her studies. But as busy as she was, she managed to balance the demands of academia with the joys of motherhood.

Jane became an integral part of Ruth's daily routine, and she credits time spent playing with Jane as a toddler as essential to her success. After attending classes all day, she'd return home for "children's hour"—a sacred break from the intensity of law school, which rejuvenated her ahead of a long night poring over her books.

As Jane grew up, she had so much exposure to her mother's passion for the law that she said it became the "fifth member" of their family. At one point when Jane was in high school, Ruth started seeking her daughter's advice on her legal briefs. She saw it more as a teaching opportunity than out of necessity, as Ruth had high expectations for her kids. Jane recalls her mother being an unsympathetic editor of her work, making her rewrite whole paragraphs several times if they didn't meet her standards (Shen, 2019).

Jane internalized Ruth's deep respect for the legal profession and developed a desire to follow in her mother's footsteps. Like her mother, Jane was an excellent student, earning her Juris Doctor from Harvard Law School, where she served as an editor of the Harvard Law Review. She later became a professor of law at the Columbia Law School, making her and Ruth the first-ever mother-daughter pair to serve on the same law faculty in America.

While Ruth's career took her to the heights of the American judicial system, Jane pursued the realm of intellectual property law, where her expertise has made her a sought-after authority in the field. But like her mother, she has been a tireless advocate for justice and equality, using her platform to champion the rights of creators and artists while also promoting a balanced approach to intellectual property protection. Her work is becoming more important than ever with the advent of AI and determining who owns the output of images and content produced by generative AI tools like ChatGPT.

Like Ruth, Jane has a son and a daughter. And just as Celia passed her unwavering commitment to the pursuit of knowledge on to Ruth, she passed it on to Jane, who kept the tradition alive by passing it on to her daughter Clara. As if fate would allow her to do anything else, Clara has continued the fight for women's rights after graduating from Harvard Law and later joining the National Women's Law Center as Senior Counsel.

Ruth's life, including parts of Jane's childhood and teenage years, were depicted onscreen in the 2018 legal drama *On the Basis of Sex*. The film was written by Ruth's nephew and produced by several members of the Ginsburg clan. Ruth even made a brief cameo while Jane's son, the actor Paul Spera, had a small part. It's an inspiring movie and highly recommended now that you've read her story.

*Knowing how chic Baria is and how she and her daughter have become style icons, it's hard to imagine Amal as a young girl not being tempted to try on her mom's shoes.

Chapter 9:

Clara Jobs

Knowing I was adopted may have made me feel more independent, but I have never felt abandoned. I've always felt special.

Steve Jobs

The Visionary Mentor

This enigmatic figure, hailed as a pioneer of technology, emerged as one of the most forward-thinking and influential visionaries of our time. With a mind as creative as it was critical, and a legacy as iconic as a bitten fruit, this agent of change revolutionized the tech industry, overcoming challenges to shape the world we know today. As the co-founder of Apple Computers and former chairman of Pixar Animations, Steve Jobs was among the most successful and richest people on the planet. He was a visionary entrepreneur who brought a new sense of innovation to the tech industry. Steve's innovative spirit gave birth to transformative products including the iPod, which not only changed the way we interact with technology but also reshaped entire industries. What's more, his legendary keynote presentations became iconic cultural events, captivating audiences with his charisma and unveiling products that became instant cultural phenomena. Steve's visionary leadership and relentless pursuit of perfection have left an enduring legacy that continues to inspire generations of entrepreneurs and creators worldwide.

Yet, he had to overcome many hurdles in life to develop his foundation and create the mindset that would help him build his empire. Were it not for his adoptive mother, Clara Jobs, Steve might not have come even close to developing the aesthetically pleasing technology that millions of people around the world use daily.

Steve was just a baby when Clara and her husband adopted him, and together the couple helped him push through the many challenges he faced, particularly at elementary school, where he would act out due to feeling unstimulated by his schoolwork. Clara helped guide Steve but gave him the freedom to create the platform from which he could pursue his entrepreneurship and step out of his comfort zone to create excellence.

Clara Jobs' Journey and Influence

Clara was born in 1924 in New Jersey to Armenian immigrants who moved to America to escape genocide in their country of birth. After finishing school, she started working as an accountant and got married to her first love. Shortly after their marriage, her first husband was killed in action during World War II.

In 1946, she married again. This time her husband was Paul Jobs, an engine mechanic who had just been discharged from the Coast Guard after also serving in the war. After moving to San Francisco, he became a car salesman. Not long after they tied the knot, Clara got pregnant. Unfortunately, they lost the baby due to an ectopic pregnancy. After that, they tried for nine years to get pregnant again but were unsuccessful. Her doctor eventually referred her to a doctor in San Francisco who cared for unwed mothers, where they applied to adopt a baby.

Not long after that, Steve was born. His biological mother was Joanne Carole Schieble, a 22-year-old graduate student at the University of Wisconsin, and his biological father was Abdulfattah Jandali, a Muslim doctorate student in political science and Joanne's teaching assistant. Joanne's Catholic family didn't approve of their relationship and threatened to withhold financial support should she continue with her relationship or have the baby. Joanne decided to give her baby up for adoption, with one condition: The adoptive parents had to have a college qualification. Initially, a wealthy Catholic lawyer and his wife were selected to adopt Joanne's baby. However, after Steve was born, they pulled out of the adoption arrangement as their preference was to adopt a baby girl.

This unexpected development left Joanne in a precarious position. Since the baby had already been born, they had to find new parents quickly. On paper, Paul and Clara wouldn't make the cut to adopt the baby as they weren't college-educated nor had money. At first, Joanne refused to sign the documents allowing the Jobs couple to adopt her baby. Only after Paul and Clara gave assurance that they would send the baby to college did she agree. When Steve was two years old, they adopted again, this time a baby girl named Patty. Paul and Clara were married for 40 years until she passed away in 1986.

Fostering Creativity and Innovation

From a young age, Paul and Clara were open with Steve about his adoption and Clara made sure he understood how special he was to them. During an interview, Steve explained, "They said, 'We specifically picked you out.'" The emphasis that his parents put on this sentence helped him to never feel abandoned. "My parents made me feel special. They were my parents. 1000%" (Daly, 2017).

As Steve grew up, he met Joanne as well as his biological sister, a daughter that Joanne and Abdulfattah had during their brief marriage years after Steve was born. He had a deep desire to meet his biological mother for two reasons: First, he wanted to make sure she was okay, and second, he wanted to thank her for not aborting him. "She was 23 and she went through a lot to have me," Steve explained (Daly, 2017). He chose to never meet his biological father, Abdulfattah. Steve is quoted as referring to Joanne and Abdulfattah as only a sperm and an egg bank. "It's not rude, it is the truth" (Isaacson, 2011).

Steve would spend hours with his dad in the garage where he learned everything about fixing cars. Even though Steve was never really interested in working on cars, he learned a lot during this time. One of the most important lessons Steve learned from his dad was to make sure you do things right; even the parts you can't see in the completed project must be perfect.

While Paul fostered Steve's interest in electronics, Clara's influence in his life was undeniable. She taught him to read before he went to kindergarten and introduced him to neighbors who sparked his interest in how simple, neat designs can bring amazing innovation, which is what he built his Apple empire on.

Even though Steve grew up to become a brilliant inventor, Clara had her hands full raising her curious and active son. When he was just a toddler, she had to rush Steve to the hospital twice: Once for ingesting poison and the second time for burning his hand after pushing a metal pin into an electric plug.

While at school, Clara constantly had to put out fires caused by her mischievous son. "I was kind of bored for the first few years, so I occupied myself by getting into trouble," Steve explained (Stevenson, 2021). He created a false poster advertising a "bring your pet to school day." Chaos broke out when the children's pets chased each other around in the school halls.

He convinced the children to tell him the combination of their bicycle locks. Then, he switched the locks around, resulting in the children struggling until very late in the evening to get their bicycles unlocked before they could go home. He also released a snake in his biology classroom and created a small explosion in his physics teacher's class.

Where most parents would punish their child for creating these pranks, Clara partially blamed the school for not challenging her son enough. As a result, Clara didn't punish him for his behavior and tried to find other ways for him to learn. When the school suggested that Steve skip two grades, Clara supported the decision and moved her young son to high school. It was at this school that he met Steve Wozniak, his partner and co-founder of the Apple Computer Company.

Even though Steve Wozniak was five years older than Steve, Clara encouraged her son to collaborate with him and even allowed them to first work from Steve's bedroom and then the family's garage.

Clara also taught her son a valuable life lesson: To always stick to the promises you make. Exactly 17 years after promising Joanne that she would make sure Steve gets a college qualification, Clara enrolled Steve in college to further his education. However, after attending a few classes, Steve decided to drop out. The college he went to was too expensive for his working-class parents and he didn't feel that it would be right to use all their savings just on his college tuition. He didn't know what he wanted to do with his life and knew that wasting his parents' hard-earned money at college wouldn't help him figure it out.

Steve came to the conclusion that he should drop out of college, which was "pretty scary at the time," but he had to "trust that it would all work out." In the end, he claimed, "It was one of the best decisions I ever made" (Strauss, 2011).

Steve died in 2011 at the age of 56 after a long and courageous battle with a rare form of pancreatic cancer. His passing was a significant loss for the technology industry and the world at large, with the news of his death met with an outpouring of grief and tributes from around the world. From tech enthusiasts to everyday consumers, people mourned the loss of a visionary who had transformed the way we interact with technology and experience the digital world.

The Ripple Effect of Clara's Influence on Steve Jobs' Success

Steve's legacy as a pioneering innovator and a true icon of the 21st century will continue to inspire and influence generations to come.

Sean Parker, co-founder of Napster and first president of Facebook, posted a heartfelt tribute to Steve Jobs, highlighting Steve as his personal hero and the inspiration behind his entrepreneurial journey. Sean described him as "the most important technology leader of our era—perhaps even the most important business leader of our era." Sean, who never met Steve, expressed his deep admiration for his creative drive, vision, and ability to change the world through sheer force of will and energy. He also noted that Steve's life and work had inspired him to pursue his own path in technology and entrepreneurship (Kroll, 2011).

One-time Google executive chairman, Eric Schmidt, declared in an interview that his hero was Steve Jobs, and that, considering the profound influence Steve had on the world, we should all strive to emulate even a fraction of his remarkable achievements.

It wouldn't take much effort to fill this chapter with more tributes to Steve Jobs and the positive impact he made to people's lives. Indeed, a whole book could be written about all the people who consider Steve Jobs as their hero. That's not to say Steve was perfect. When one of his most famous and successful fans met Steve for the first and only time at a party, he recalls Steve being "kind of a jerk" to him. Yet, this encounter didn't discourage Elon Musk's admiration for the great man.

The reason for including these tributes to Steve Jobs is to really drive home just how freakin' huge his impact was, not just on the tech industry, but on brilliant minds and innovators everywhere. Sure, Steve had his jerk moments and wasn't perfect by any stretch. But at the end of the day, his unwavering intensity, his maniacal attention to detail, his ability to blend art and technology into something trendsetting and beautiful—that struck awe into the hearts of visionaries and entrepreneurs alike.

But before he made a dent in the universe, Steve's mother was there from the very beginning, shaping his mindset and driving forces in profound ways. Without Clara seeding that demanding spirit at his core, it's hard to imagine Steve could have cultivated the intensity, perfectionistic attention to detail, and visionary foresight that made him such a tsunami of influence.

Breaking with Tradition to Create Innovative Things

While not every impulsive or mischievous kid grows up to change the world like Steve Jobs, it's extraordinary to discover just how many of the world's most celebrated people have similar histories (see the next chapter on Leah Adler, mother of Steven Spielberg, for example). A common thread crucial to their future success was their mothers' talent for finding ways to channel their boundless energy and insatiable curiosity in positive directions.

That's not to say that these pioneers were steered into what most people would consider a conventional path. In Steve's case, Clara saw how bored Steve was with a traditional school setting and how it made him act out. This led her to support the decision to skip grades and transition to a more stimulating environment at high school. She later supported Steve's decision to drop out of college, understanding that it wasn't the right fit for him. For Steven Spielberg, his mother would let him take "sick days" from school and go help him live out his filmmaking fantasies. And when Lorna Finman saw the potential in her son, Erik, that traditional schooling failed to nurture, she drew on the same wisdom and flexibility shown by Clara and Leah to allow her son to tailor his specific educational needs and let his talents flourish.

Lorna Finman is an accomplished physicist, with a PhD from Stanford University. She once had a major role in NASA's space program during the 80s. Interestingly, she was supposed to be part of the ill-fated Challenger crew but couldn't go because she was pregnant with Erik's older brother at the time. Lorna's love for the stars instilled in her three sons a desire to get involved in science from an early age.

Like Steve Jobs, Erik Finman showed an independent streak and distaste for traditional schooling from a young age. At just 12 years old, he made a deal with his parents that if he became a millionaire by age 18 then they wouldn't force him to go to college. And so, armed with knowledge of an emerging disruptive technology and $1,000 his grandmother gave him to go towards his education, he set out to fulfil his end of the deal. The result? Erik's investment in Bitcoin when it was just $12 per coin had grew to over $1 million by age 16. Good to her word, Lorna let Erik skip college. But thanks to his new-found wealth and an increasing confidence in himself, Erik actually dropped out of high school, moved out of his parents house, and began a new life in Palo Alto, California, where he lived predominantly on his bitcoin investments and income he made from companies he started, sold, and invested in.

"High school sucked. I hated it. I felt like I wasn't learning anything useful and that I was wasting my time," reflected Erik on his schooling (Madell, 2021). Erik even had a teacher tell him that he wouldn't amount to anything and to prepare for a future working at McDonalds. In spite of his bad experience, he admits that education has value for those suited to use what they learn in school, although much of what he defines as useful in today's society can be learned online for free. His mother more or less agrees with Erik's assessment and believes that everyone has a unique learning style and therefore should have an educational system to match. Boasting an MIT-educated robotics wiz, a Johns Hopkins-educated software entrepreneur, and a multi-millionaire as her sons, few could argue with her.

Despite their non-traditional paths in education, the mothers of Steve and Erik nurtured their son's talents while backing their desire to buck conventions. Steering away from a prescribed route gave them the freedom to explore and chase their passions, and Clara and Lorna were there reassuring them when they went against the grain of societal expectations.

Chapter 10:

Leah Adler

Mine was not a conventional childhood at all. For one thing, my mother and father were madly in love with each other their whole lives, and I thought that's how everybody lived.

Leah Adler

The Maestro of Passion

From heartwarming tales that tug at the heartstrings to edge-of-your-seat thrillers, this cinematic genius has brought to life stories of extraterrestrial friendships, dinosaur escapades, and harrowing wartime missions. Steven Spielberg is arguably one of the most famous film directors in modern Hollywood, being the driving force behind blockbuster hits such as *E.T.*, *Jurassic Park*, *The Color Purple*, *Saving Private Ryan*, and countless other award-winning creations. Steven's use of backlighting has been deemed groundbreaking, his unique use of color celebrated, and his war movie realism captivating. His career has spanned over 40 years, and he continues to set the gold standard in filmmaking.

Yet, no matter the accolades and praise he receives, Steven remains humble and talks openly about the details of his work. He's also quick to attribute the foundation of his success back to his mother, Leah Adler, and acknowledge the remarkable influence she had on his life. Leah played a crucial role in fostering his love for filmmaking and steering him toward becoming one of Hollywood's most accomplished directors. She instilled in her son the desire not to explicitly pursue a career of wealth but rather to follow his passions in everything he did.

Leah Adler's Journey and Influence

Leah was born in 1920 in Cincinnati, Ohio, to a public speaker mother and a Russian immigrant father, who never officially worked. The free time he had available resulted in a beautiful father-daughter bond. They did many exciting things, which helped Leah see life from a different perspective.

Her mother, on the other hand, was anything but domesticated. She would walk around the house reciting her speeches while she was doing her chores, such as cleaning and dusting. However, since her focus was on getting every word in her speech right, she would often miss large speckles of dust. "She was a marvelous lady who never mastered the can opener in her whole life," Leah explained (Bernstein, 1990).

Due to her mother being the only breadwinner, the family grew up poor. To make matters worse, they were living in the Great Depression, a time known for the economic downturn in many countries. However, Leah was adamant that this didn't affect them negatively. "There was no depression in our house. We didn't know what we didn't have." This gave her a bigger appreciation and excitement for the things that she did have. One night after getting new shoes, she would jump out of bed throughout the night to admire her new shoes. "Now that I can have everything, I've lost that" (Bernstein, 1990).

Leah fell in love with the sound of a piano at the age of five. She went on to become a concert pianist but gave this up when she married engineer Arnold Spielberg and moved to Arizona. The couple had four children: Steven and his three sisters Sue, Anne, and Nancy. She also had a degree in home economics and was an accomplished painter.

There were many days when the family had no food to eat. Steven's father would buy and sell old jewelry to try to make ends meet. Regardless of how difficult their circumstances might have been, they chose to see life in a positive way. During an interview, Leah told of a time when he made $10 selling jewelry. "He came home and said, 'We're going on vacation.' And we did. That's faith" (Bernstein, 1990).

After Leah and Arnold's divorce, she moved her young children to California where she met and married Bernard Adler. Together, they opened a kosher restaurant. Leah died in 2017 at the age of 97.

Inspiring Artistic Talent and Vision

Leah openly spoke about how challenging it was to raise Steven and explained that his unique abilities showed early on. While it was clear that he was talented, Leah was often frustrated by Steven's inability to finish the projects he started. He once wanted to paint the neighbor's tree trunks white, but only painted three of them. When he committed to painting the bathroom, he gave up after painting the toilet and mirror. Leah recalled during an interview that when his teacher once told her that Steve was a special boy, she couldn't decide how to interpret the teacher's meaning. Instead of being a cuddly young boy, Steve was more on the scary side of things, constantly teasing and pranking everyone around him, including his sisters. "He used to stand outside their windows at night, howling, 'I am the moon…' They're still scared of the moon. And he cut off the head of one of Nancy's dolls and served it to her" (Bernstein, 1990).

Although she was raised in an orthodox Jewish home, Leah moved away from this religion and chose to raise her children in a Gentile neighborhood. She believes this was one of her biggest mistakes, as it resulted in her children being mocked and called "dirty Jews." Unlike Leah, Steven couldn't just accept the insults and avoid confrontation. Instead, he got revenge by smearing peanut butter on all their windows (Bernstein, 1990).

Once he joined the Boy Scouts, he could use his pranking nature for good in completing his merit badge for moviemaking. His parents bought him a video camera and some equipment, which soon took over the décor in their home. On other days, he would load Leah's car with equipment and costumes and have the whole family go with him to a location where he would direct them to act out short scenes.

He completed his first full-length movie called *Firelight* when he was only 14 years old and convinced a local movie theater to show it. Leah helped to advertise the showing, thinking that she was helping her son enjoy his hobby. Little did she know he would actually make money from that first showing. After that, there was no stopping Steven, and their whole community bought into Steven's clear talent. When he wanted to do a shoot inside a hospital, the hospital management closed an entire wing for him to use. And, when he wanted to do a shoot at an airport, the management there let him use an entire runway. "Nobody ever said no to Steven," recalled Leah (Bernstein, 1990).

This is evident in the complete mess she allowed her talented young son to make in her kitchen. He wanted to film something oozing out of Leah's kitchen cabinets. To help him create this, she bought 30 cans of cherries and cooked them until the cherry cans exploded. During an interview, she half-joked that for many years after that incident, she was still wiping cherry residue from the kitchen counters.

His passion for filmmaking at a young age confirmed Leah's mother's beliefs that there was something special about her grandson. "My mother always used to say. 'The world is going to hear of this boy.' I used to think she said it so I wouldn't kill him" (Bernstein, 1990).

Steven was still a teenager when he spent his days at Universal Studios, pretending to work there. He eventually sold his first script and used his proceeds to buy Leah a TV, the first of many presents. "He spoils me rotten, like I spoiled him," she said (Bernstein, 1990).

He often relied on his mother's musical input when scoring a movie. Even though Leah knew he didn't truly need her musical advice on his films, she was happy to go along with it to be part of his life and work.

Steven took inspiration from his own life and upbringing in making two of his biggest movies, *E.T. the Extra-Terrestrial* and *The Fabelmans*. *E.T.*, released in 1982, was inspired by his parent's divorce and the impact this separation had on him and his younger sisters. He explained that when parents get divorced, there is naturally greater responsibility on the children, particularly the older siblings who feel like they should play a helping role in taking care of the younger ones. This is the role that Elliott in the film portrays in taking care of both his little sister and the alien. "I had been working on an actual literal script about my parents' separation and... what it did to my sisters and myself" (Juneau & Huver, 2022).

The Fabelmans, released in 2022, was written to be a companion piece to *E.T.* in that it deals with the family secrets that ultimately can lead to a divorce. It's based on a secret that Steven kept with Leah until her death: When he was 16 years old, he discovered that Leah was having an affair with a close family friend, Bernard Adler, whom she eventually married. Before her death, Leah gave Steven her blessing to make this movie.

Like Leah, the main character in this movie, Mitzi, is a musician who loved art but gave up her aspirations of making a career out of her music to raise her four children. Steven said that his mother's nature of always wanting the most that life could possibly offer her, helped push his own ambitious nature and made him believe that he could become whatever he wanted to be.

Steven has publicly called his mother his lucky charm, and this feeling was mutual. Until the day of her death, she was a proud mother. "I told Steve, if I'd known how famous he was going to be, I'd have had my uterus bronzed," she was quoted (Barnes, 2017).

The Ripple Effect of Leah's Influence on Steven Spielberg's Success

Leah's influence on Steven can be seen in many of his projects. Whether it's his unique take on his parent's divorce in *E.T.* or an actual retelling of his childhood experiences in *The Fabelmans*, or even the musical accompaniments on his movies, there's a lot of Leah in his work. Leah bought Steven his first video-making equipment and allowed him to explore his creativity without limits—something he took to heart and continues to do.

Remember the emotional support she gave him to start his filmmaking journey? Well, Leah also helped Steven take time off school to go film his projects by writing sick notes.

Like many of the mothers featured in this book, Leah recognized that her son had to be encouraged to develop his passions at a time when he's passionate about them and allow his imagination to break free or else the moment and his future successes could be lost forever. When we look for the greater impact Steven has had on the world, it's so easy to find examples of the colossal influence he exerts on his peers and the industry at large. In researching this section, there were a number of directions it could've taken. In the end, I decided to show a few different ways Steven's imagination in filmmaking influences others that exclude simply how to shoot their own films. Doing so conveys just how boundless Leah allowed Steven's imagination to roam.

First, Steven understands that music is a powerful emotional tool that can evoke a range of emotions in an audience. In *Schindler's List*, the haunting violin theme captures the tragedy of the Holocaust. The uplifting notes in *Close Encounters of the Third Kind* evoke wonder and curiosity as humans encounter extraterrestrial life. Much more than something nice to hear in the background, Steven understands that music is an integral part of the storytelling, teaching aspiring filmmakers to use music to enhance emotional moments, build tension, and create lasting impressions.

Second, Steven embraces cutting-edge technology. In 1993, he unleashed *Jurassic Park* upon the world. The film had to include dinosaurs when there weren't any to film. To that end, he embraced CGI to create lifelike, computer-generated creatures that roared, stomped, and terrified audiences—it was a seismic shift in visual effects. Suddenly, the impossible became possible, and filmmakers realized that CGI could transport viewers to unimaginable realms.

Last, but certainly not least, Steven's movies inspire fashion trends. Just as music can enhance a feeling of adventure and exploration, so too can the distinctive fedora hat and brown leather jacket worn by Indiana Jones. Steven understands the role clothing plays in giving visual references and revealing character depth. Remember, it wasn't Leah who loaded up her car with costumes for a day of shooting, it was young Steven.

Guiding but Staying Open-minded

Leah Adler took encouragement of young Steven's hobbies beyond providing emotional support and buying beginner equipment. She took inspired steps to carve out time for him to work on his craft—ok, technically he should've been at school working on his education. She even played parts in front of the camera while shooting films on his "sick days". But no-one could fault his mother for encouraging his unique abilities and giving him every chance possible to turn a passionate hobby into a profession.

Steven Spielberg's story in some ways echoes that of Kate Hudson. She may not be a changemaker on the same level as Steven, but she's certainly very influential after having dipped her toes into almost every aspect of show business. In addition to being an acclaimed actress, Kate has also tried her hand in producing as well as entrepreneurship as the owner of the activewear line Fabletics. But those aren't the reasons for comparing her to Steven. Rather, Kate was similarly raised by a charismatic mother who also had to find a more productive outlet for her child's disruptive behavior. What's more, their mothers were already very familiar with the film industry and knew the best ways to teach their kids on how to navigate it.

The daughter of Bill Hudson and Goldie Hawn, Kate had an early introduction to the entertainment industry. Aside from her immense acting talent, Kate's success is thought to be significantly facilitated by her mother Goldie, whose mindful and open-minded approach to parenting has set Kate on the path of success.

To say that Goldie is a Hollywood veteran would be an understatement. Perhaps it's even more fascinating that Goldie had the unique talent to transfer all of the authenticity and an artistic outlook on life onto her parenting style. In fact, a strong connection to her daughter Kate remains as relevant a staple in Goldie's resume as her career. Goldie is known to be a caring, supportive mother, who gave as much of herself as she could to raise her daughter.

Goldie was born in 1945 in Washington to a Jewish mother and a Presbyterian father. Her maternal grandparents were Hungarian immigrants. From a young age, Goldie was a performer. She started taking ballet and tap dance lessons at the age of three, and, by the time she was 10, she performed on stage in a production of *The Nutcracker*. Two years later, she had her acting debut in *Romeo and Juliet* at the Virginia Shakespeare Festival. By the time she turned 19, she dropped out of college where she was majoring in drama to be a professional dancer and run a ballet school.

She married her first husband, director Gus Trikonis, in 1968, but the couple split after five years. In 1975, Goldie got married again, this time to musician Bill Hudson. They had two children together, Oliver and Kate. Again, her marriage ended in divorce. Since 1983, she has shared her life with actor Kurt Russel, with whom she shares a son Wyatt. The couple has repeatedly said although they share their lives together, they have no plans to get married.

Goldie has opened up about suffering from severe anxiety as a young girl, particularly after watching a war movie for school. For months after that, she had nightmares that the Russians would bomb them. After some time, her anxiety attacks started to subside, until she started to perform on a TV show. Suddenly, she was that scared little girl again and when she had to step outside of her room (her comfort zone), she felt like vomiting. "I didn't know why I was feeling anxious or what was wrong with me... while I was supposedly becoming something that everyone was so excited for me" (Todisco, 2019).

While seeking help for her mental health, Goldie was advised to meditate to find happiness. This made her understand the amazing power her mind had and if she wanted to fix anything in her life, her mind was the best place to start. She decided on meditation as that was one of the more popular methods of dealing with mental health problems such as anxiety in her community. Once she got started, meditation gave her amazing joyful experiences. "I felt like I returned back to my deepest part, to my heart, to my joy. It just hit this seed of joy that I always had as a young girl. Because all I ever wanted to be was happy" (Todisco, 2019).

Since her mental health played such a big role in her childhood, she founded The Goldie Hawn Foundation, which developed the Mind Up program. The program teaches children to regulate their emotions, manage their stress, and approach their struggles with compassion. She wants children to understand that they don't always have to rely only on medication to treat their illnesses. While there are many instances where medication might be absolutely necessary, these children are also taught to calm themselves down and that they are in control of their own lives and emotions. "I just want to see kids smile and live safely," Goldie explained (Todisco, 2019).

Growing up in a house with two major Hollywood actors as parents, it's only natural that Kate and both her brothers found themselves auditioning at castings for roles and making it big. But with Kate, Goldie didn't wait for roles to come to her daughter naturally. She directly influenced her daughter's career by sending her to do an apprenticeship at the Williamstown Theater Festival in Massachusetts in an effort to get her away from boys. Kate recalls that even though she enjoyed working in an acting environment and on her craft, she didn't want to spend her holiday working when she could have fun with her friends. However, Kate learned so much during her time then that she now believes that was one of the best things Goldie could've done for her daughter.

Over the span of her career, Goldie would often give Kate advice, particularly when it came to role selection. This resulted in Kate turning down the lead role for *10 Things I Hate About You*, as Goldie felt the script could've read better. While she has created a successful career in her own right, she never tried to compare herself or her career to her mother. "There's no emulating mama's career. She's an original. She's an icon," Kate explained (Weinberg, 2022).

Kate also pulled a lot of parenting inspiration from Goldie in how she mothers her own three children, sons Ryder and Bing, and daughter Rani Rose.

During an interview with People, Kate said that Goldie has always been her greatest cheerleader and so available for her young daughter that she could only hope to be able to give her own daughter that same level of confidence. Goldie added to this, that there is a "domino effect" of parenting because when you raise your own children, you're teaching them how to be parents, as well, which is "a tremendous responsibility." Hawn believes that the keys to her strong bonds with her children were created by loving them, listening to them, paying attention to their lives, being there, and focusing on their needs. That, and cooking for them and laughing as much as possible (Weaver, 2024).

Kate is full of praise for the mothering role that Goldie played in her life, particularly since Kate's three children all have different fathers, and Goldie and Kate's father had split. As a result, Goldie had a fantastic opportunity to teach her daughter to respect your co-parent, whether you're in a relationship with them or not. Kate says that no matter what happened or how Goldie might have felt at that moment, she would never speak ill about Kate's father. As a result, when any of Kate's friends ever speak badly about their co-partners or former spouses, she gets highly upset as they don't realize how negative words or resentment can affect their children. "No matter what, I never heard a bad word about my father. It's not our place to tell [kids] how to feel about the other parents," Kate said (Weaver, 2024).

The mothers of Steven and Kate played a massive role in setting them up for success when it looked like their unruly behavior was taking them down a different path. Leah and Goldie guided them towards their careers but allowed them the freedom to explore their creative efforts on their own.

Chapter 11:

Maye Musk

When the kids were growing up, they learned to be independent. I told them, "As long as you're doing something good, it's worth pursuing."

Maye Musk

Balancing Passion and Purpose

This South African-born billionaire has become a household name, founding and running groundbreaking companies that are reshaping industries and pushing the boundaries of what's possible. From revolutionizing the automotive sector with sleek, eco-friendly cars to launching rockets with the goal of colonizing Mars, this visionary entrepreneur has captured the world's attention with his ambitious projects. His relentless pursuit of innovation and his larger-than-life persona have made him one of the most influential and controversial figures of our time.

From a very young age, there was something special about Elon Musk. He stood out due to his keen interest in acquiring knowledge. Apart from his extreme and obvious intelligence, Elon had another important factor in his support system: A mother he could model and who would support him in creating his own path in life.

Had it not been for Maye's influence on his life, Elon might not have reached the amazing success that propelled him to become one of the richest people in the world.

Maye Musk's Journey and Influence

Maye's life story reads like the plot of a movie. Born in 1948 in Saskatchewan, Canada, she is a twin and one of five children of well-to-do parents. She immigrated to South Africa with her family when she was only two years old.

As self-styled adventurers, her parents would often take their children on trips off the beaten track, like when they spent three weeks trekking across the Kalahari Desert and sleeping on the sand in search of the Lost City. They enjoyed it so much they repeated the trip every year for almost a decade. Or the time her dad flew them all from South Africa to Australia in a single-engine plane, without a radio or GPS—the only people to have ever done that.

Maye's parents encouraged her and her siblings to never be afraid to try new things. She learned through their example what it meant to be adventurous and have a sense of independence. The children also learned the value of hard work thanks to their entrepreneurial parents, with Maye helping to prepare newsletters and monthly bulletins for their latest endeavor. She was 8 at the time. And by 12, she worked alongside her twin sister as a receptionist for their father.

Her modeling career started when she was 15, learning the trade at the modeling school of her mother's friend and working mainly on weekends doing catalog and runway shoots. When a friend entered her in a modeling contest a few years later, she won. It gave her the confidence to enter the 1969 Miss South Africa contest, in which she was a finalist.

After completing school and qualifying as a dietician, she married whom she thought would be her Prince Charming, the South African Errol Musk, only for him to turn out to be a "pig" who she claims abused her during their relationship (Tremaine, 2023). She had three children with Errol: Sons Elon and Kimbal, and daughter Tosca. After a nine-year marriage filled with many challenges, Maye and Errol got divorced. This resulted in Maye becoming a single mother who had to work hard to make ends meet. As Maye explained, "He (Errol) was very rich but made sure I had nothing" (Tremaine, 2023).

For the first few years after the divorce, Elon chose to live with his father to keep him from feeling lonely and only saw his mother every other weekend for a visit. He is now vocal about this being one of the worst decisions of his life, calling Errol a "terrible human being" (Murphy, 2021).

Once all her children were back under her roof, there was even more pressure on Maye to meet their basic needs. This caused her high levels of anxiety. She told *People* that after her divorce and starting over in Canada, where she had taken the children without her frozen assets in South Africa and without local modeling contacts, her biggest fear was being unable to provide for her children (2023). To this end, she worked five jobs to make ends meet, including as a dietitian, a researcher at the university, a teacher at a nutrition college, a model, and the owner of her own modeling agency.

This drive to provide for her family propelled her in her careers as a model, dietitian, and author to such an extent that she built a very healthy net worth for herself. Her 2019 memoir sold incredibly well, especially in China where she's held in high esteem by Chinese women who also want to have children and a career while being a woman of elegance and sophistication. In 2022 at the age of 74, she became the oldest model to ever appear on the cover of the swimsuit edition of *Sports Illustrated* magazine. Maye's modeling career has now spanned six decades, which is a remarkable achievement given most models find their careers over by their mid-20s.

Maye's success in different careers proved to her children the importance of hard work, responsibility, and doing what you can to help your family. You'll also notice she only worked jobs she had an interest in. Most people trying to keep a roof over their kid's heads and put food on the table would take any job going, but not Maye. She knew what she wanted, knew what her skills were, and was always determined to make things happen. These are all traits she learned from her parents, and heavily influenced the way she raised her own children, inspiring and supporting each of them to be the makers of their own destinies.

For instance, knowing Elon was into technology, she bought him a computer when she was able to afford one. He's now at the helm of several of the world's biggest tech companies. In Kimbal's case, she let him take the lead when grocery shopping and cooking for the family as was his passion at the time. He now runs his own chain of restaurants and a nonprofit organization helping to get more fresh produce into underserved schools. And as for Tosca, Maye would spend hours watching movies with her. She later founded her own company taking romance novels and turning them into films.

Encouraging Ambition and Embracing Challenges

Despite being a good role model for her children, Maye's parenting style goes against the advice that some parenting experts would give. Instead of guiding her children through every challenge of life, Maye stood back and allowed her children the freedom to choose the path they believed would be best for them. This wasn't entirely out of choice, but also necessity.

As a single mother she had to work long hours in multiple jobs to provide for her three children. As a result, her children had to grow up very fast and accept responsibility for their own lives, which included making sure their own homework was done properly. If their teacher scolded them for not handing in their homework, then it was their fault, not Maye's. The freedom Maye allowed her children in choosing their paths fostered a sense of responsibility and independence, crucial traits for their later achievements.

Elon and his siblings may have had a wealthy father, but they certainly didn't grow up in riches. Maye insists that due to the fact her children weren't used to living in luxury, being poor didn't affect them negatively. She believes this is where many parents make their biggest parenting mistake: Instead of focusing on teaching their youngsters good manners and allowing them to take responsibility for their own lives and future, they stress over their children and the luxuries they want to give them. Maye's belief that adversity does not define your future but rather strengthens character is a lesson that undoubtedly influenced Elon's approach to challenges.

While this advice might not work for all children, it certainly did for Elon, who showed signs of genius from a very young age. He taught himself to read, not for fun but to acquire knowledge. As a result, he was sent to school at a younger age than what was typically the case for children in South Africa. Since he was both the youngest and the smallest in his class, he would often be the focus of bullies.

In one bullying incident, he was beat up so bad that he had to undergo plastic surgery to fix the damage, particularly to rebuild his broken nose. His father often sided with the bullies and even looked for mistakes in Elon's behavior that might have instigated the attacks. Maye, however, provided the support that young Elon desperately needed, which eventually included moving him to a different school and ensuring these attacks didn't keep him from excelling. This pivotal moment in Elon's childhood, supported by his mother's encouragement, marked the beginning of his journey to becoming a visionary entrepreneur.

He was only 12 years old when he created a computer game by himself. As many parents would be, Maye was very impressed with her son's creativity and innovation, and she showed the game to engineering students at the local university. When they were also dazzled by the game, she encouraged Elon to enter it into a competition held by a magazine, which he subsequently won. Maye believes that the organizers of the competition never knew he was only 12 years old.

This early success and clear signs of brilliance didn't eliminate Maye's worries over her timid son. "Because many geniuses end up in a basement being a genius but not applying it," Maye was quoted (Todisco, 2021). When Elon, together with his younger brother Kimbal Musk, founded their first company, Zip2, which provided an online city guide and directions, Maye let out a sigh of relief. In fact, she was so impressed with their innovation that she invested in her young sons' company.

After they sold this company, Elon's entrepreneurial spirit went into overdrive: He first saw a gap in the banking industry and developed PayPal. Then, he started doing research on space, electric cars, and solar energy, and couldn't decide which industry to disrupt next. "I said just choose one, and of course, he didn't listen to me," Maye told People (Todisco, 2021).

Elon is arguably the world's most successful entrepreneur, having founded or having a major role in founding several companies that have revolutionized industries, including the aforementioned Zip2 and PayPal, electric car manufacturer, Tesla, the space company, SpaceX, the developer of implantable brain-computer interfaces, Neuralink, the tunneling venture, Boring Company, and the creator of the wildly popular ChatGPT, OpenAI. He also has high aspirations for X (formerly Twitter), which he bought in 2022.

Elon's approach to work is nothing short of intense. He routinely clocks in up to 100 hours a week, with reports of up to 120 hours during crunch times. Like it was for Maye, it's all about passion and purpose. His projects aren't just business ventures; they align with his personal interests and fuel his relentless drive.

The Ripple Effect of Maye's Influence on Elon Musk's Success

The ripple effect of Maye's influence doesn't end with Elon. The mindset he developed from watching her, a mindset that views problems as opportunities for growth and innovation rather than obstacles, has inspired a generation to dream big. He's not afraid to tackle some of the most daunting challenges facing humanity, like sustainable energy and visiting Mars. In fact, when anyone in the Musk clan is told that their ideas can't be done, they already know that they can and will be.

Maye's influence further extends to how Elon envisions the future of education. Maye holds two master of science degrees and dedicated her adult life to nutrition research. Elon obtained bachelor's degrees in economics and physics from the prestigious University of Pennsylvania, before dropping out of his PhD program in physics at Stanford after just two days.

Maye taught Elon to value education, but he doesn't see the need for a college education. Even high school has its downsides. The problem he sees with traditional schooling is that it's boring and neither engages students enough nor teaches on a personal level.

As if he wasn't busy enough already with all his business ventures and being a father of more than 10 children, Elon is redefining education through his Astra Nova School. This innovative school was originally founded to provide a bespoke education for his children and those of SpaceX employees.

Astra Nova's curriculum is centered around critical thinking, ethics, and collaboration. It's a place where real-world problems are explored, encouraging students to think deeply and ask questions. The school values hands-on learning versus memorizing facts. An example he gives is learning about wrenches from a whiteboard at the front of a classroom has less impact on a student's education than learning about wrenches as a byproduct of taking apart a car's engine.

It would've been far easier for Maye to buy engineering books for Elon when he showed interest in computing as a child. Given her financial struggles at the time, it would've been even better to have just borrowed the books from the library. But she knew he needed to learn about computers by using a computer. And now Elon is giving that same chance to many more students eager to explore their individual curiosities with personalized, hands-on learning.

Musk and Rive – Twinning and Winning

Maye's bond with twin Kaye goes beyond sharing the same DNA, enjoying the same explorative upbringing, and having names that rhyme. They got married in a double wedding, and like Maye, Kaye Rive is an entrepreneur who also raised successful entrepreneurs.

Maye and Kaye shared many adventures with their siblings. Their children had adventures of their own while growing up together in Pretoria. One early business idea the Musk-Rive cousins had was to sell Easter eggs door to door. But rather than simply buy the eggs and sell them on at a higher price, they realized they could make a lot more money making the eggs themselves by melting and reshaping cheaper, regular chocolate bars and wrapping them in some decorative foil. With manufacturing sorted, they then mapped out a strategy to sell them for about ten times the price of a store-bought Easter egg. It was a simple plan: Anyone shocked upon hearing the price was given a rehearsed speech about how the money raised goes towards supporting young capitalists.

Like Elon, Kimbal, and Tosca, the Rive siblings grew up watching their mother Kaye work long hours, which they also internalized as normal. She regularly worked 16-hour days, seven days a week on the natural-health business she ran with her husband. The countless unsupervised hours fostered the same kind of independence and determination to come up with ventures of their own. By the time they were adults, they had gained enough confidence in their abilities to take the necessary risks to achieve success.

Lyndon and Russ Rive co-founded a successful subscription-based remote management software company called Everdream, which Dell bought in 2007. Russ would then go on to co-find the innovative design company SuperUber in Brazil. Lyndon and his other brother Peter went on to co-find the largest distributed solar company in the world, SolarCity, in 2006. It was eventually acquired by Tesla in 2016.

While Maye and Kaye were busy working on their passions all day, their kids were busy building the skills needed to conquer new frontiers in diverse industries. The children thrived in their unsupervised freedom and brainstormed various schemes to make money, like selling Easter eggs around the neighborhood and opening a new local video arcade. Maye and Kaye instilled values of hard work and curiosity in their children, not by telling them, but by showing them. Adding the skills they developed in problem solving and persistence, it seems impossible they'd fail to become successful individuals.

Or were they just destined for greatness thanks to the genes of their mutual grandparents?

Chapter 12:

Debbie Phelps

You raise your children with wings to fly... But it doesn't mean you can't all hang out together.

Debbie Phelps

The Seeker of Success

Many people may be surprised to hear that this great freestyle swimmer severely disliked swimming at first. In fact, he would make a fuss every time he had to dive into the pool. Yet during his career, he bagged a record 28 Olympic medals, of which a remarkable 23 were gold. American swimmer Michael Phelps is widely regarded as one of the greatest Olympians in history.

His mother, Debbie Phelps, wouldn't let her young son give up on this sport. Even though she had no idea of the success awaiting him in the future, she understood the value swimming brought for Michael in helping him to find focus and get rid of some of his excessive energy. She remained a driving force behind her son's success, not just during the start of his career but also when he was winning one gold medal after the other.

Debbie Phelps' Journey and Influence

Debbie was born in 1951 in Baltimore, Maryland, where she has lived all her life. Her father, the family's only breadwinner, passed away when she was 20 years old. Since her mother had never worked, she suddenly had to find ways to care for her family. She watched her mother stretch her budget and turn every dollar over a few times to try to make ends meet. In doing so, Debbie learned the importance of working on a tight budget. But she never lost the ability to embrace life and have the necessary faith that you'll make it through the toughest times.

After finishing school, she obtained her degree in education and became a public school teacher in home economics. In 1973, she married her high school sweetheart Fred Phelps, and the couple had three children together, Hilary, Whitney, and Michael. They divorced when Michael was only nine years old. Debbie says the divorce took her by complete surprise, and she quickly had to adjust to her new life. Debbie and Fred grew apart completely. All three of her children chose to stay with her, resulting in Debbie having to quickly learn to juggle her work and parenting duties as a single mother.

Debbie holds a master's degree in education and, after serving as a school principal for many years, Debbie has been the executive director of the Education Foundation of the Baltimore County Public Schools, Inc., since 2012. She also penned her first memoir book, *A Mother For All Seasons*, published in 2009.

Guidance Through Obstacles to Stardom

Michael was first exposed to swimming when his two sisters started at the North Baltimore Aquatic Club. They both became accomplished swimmers, with his eldest sister Hilary swimming her way to the world championships in backstroke. While Debbie already had to juggle driving her two daughters to swimming lessons, she also had to help her son cope with the challenges of school.

Michael was nine years old when he was diagnosed with the neurodiversity attention deficit hyperactivity disorder (ADHD). He was extremely hyperactive and struggled to concentrate on his schoolwork. This meant that Debbie would constantly receive phone calls from the principal's office reporting Michael's latest antics. He would lift his desk in the middle of a lesson and run around the class while holding his desk above his shoulders. He would continue with these types of antics to entertain his friends. Eventually, Michael was diagnosed with ADHD and started taking medication to help him treat his symptoms more effectively. Once he finished middle school, he transitioned off the medication as he was struggling with peer pressure because he needed medication to make it through the school day (PSN Team, 2017).

Debbie used her training and skills as a teacher to develop routines and strategies that would help Michael cope with the challenges that his symptoms of ADHD caused. Debbie explains that she was his strongest advocate when it came to Michael's education and would talk with his teachers. When the teachers moaned that Michael wouldn't sit still, she suggested they move him to the back of the class. She helped his teachers understand that even though children who struggle with inattentiveness generally don't do well at the back of a class, it would actually help Michael as he would then be able to stand up and move around without distracting the other children when his high energy levels made it too difficult for him to remain seated.

Another strategy Debbie implemented was using sports to wear his energy levels down. Apart from swimming, Michael played baseball, ran cross-country, and took part in lacrosse. Through her innovative strategies and relentless advocacy, Debbie ensured Michael's talents were nurtured in a way that respected his unique needs and strengths.

At first, the Olympic swimmer didn't want to get close to the swimming pool. He hated to put his face in the water, so Debbie suggested he start with backstroke (Paz, 2020). One of the common symptoms of ADHD is hyperfocus, which is the ability to focus intently on something of interest. Hyperfocus can also result in time blindness, where you spend so much time hyperfocusing that you lose complete track of time. Once Michael overcame his fear of being in the water, he started to enjoy swimming so much that he could use his hyperfocus to perfect his swimming technique and spend hours in the water.

Debbie relied heavily on her support system, particularly when her children's schedules clashed. She made friends with mothers of children in the same swimming groups as her children, which gave her support when she couldn't pick them up on time. "My mother gave me a lot of willpower and determination to believe in myself and I had a strong support system that helped make sure that everything was going well," she recalled (Allen Clark, 2008).

Once her children achieved success in swimming, Debbie made sure she wouldn't fall into the trap of being a stage mom. She never pushed her children in their sport. She believed that was the job of their coaches. Instead, she focused on being their mother, not their motivator. "I couldn't get caught up in the stage mom junk. I took on the logic of Michael's coaches—it's here and then gone tomorrow," Debbie said (Allen Clark, 2008).

There were many times when Debbie felt overwhelmed by her never ending to-do list. Like a lot of single mothers, it was easy for her to get so caught up in parenting tasks that she forgot to take care of herself. Something had to change, and so, once a month, she would schedule time for herself, calling it a "Debbie Day," where she would do something that she really enjoys, whether it takes only a couple of hours or the whole day (PSN Team, 2017).

After Michael won his first Olympic gold medal in Athens in 2004, he stepped off the winner's platform and walked straight to his mother to give her a big hug of gratitude for always supporting him.

When asked what the biggest secret is to raising an Olympian, Debbie explained that it's to always ensure you don't put any unnecessary expectations or stress onto your child. Instead, she believes that parents need to relax and understand that setting high expectations of their children, particularly unrealistic ones, won't help anyone. Debbie says parents should put themselves in their children's shoes when they set expectations to make sure what they want from them is in alignment with their own hopes and ideals. Also, she believes parents should always remember that each child will develop at their own pace and, therefore, should never be compared. As Debbie puts it, "There may not be another Michael Phelps for decades, even though I have parents tell me their son is on the same track" (Poirier-Leroy, 2018).

Her efforts were both seen and appreciated by her three children. "My mom raised us single-handedly… Growing up, I learned from her example about hard work and dedication," Michael said during an interview (Wickham, 2017). Michael's acknowledgment of his mother's single-handed efforts reminds us that behind every public victory are private sacrifices and moments of support that make such achievements possible.

The Ripple Effect of Debbie's Influence on Michael Phelps' Success

Debbie Phelps cheered for Michael from the stands as a proud mother during his swimming competitions. His journey to Olympic record holder started years earlier when Debbie recognized his needs as a child with ADHD struggling to stay focused in the classroom. Things improved further when Michael got over his initial fear of being under water and found swimming as a way to hyperfocus, burn off excess energy, and ultimately, be happy. The result of Debbie's expertise as an educator and love as a mother is an individual whose influence extends far beyond the pool.

Using the $1 million bonus he received for winning a record eight gold medals at the 2008 Beijing Games, Michael kick-started the Michael Phelps Foundation (MPF)—a nonprofit organization focused on growing the sport of swimming and promoting healthy, active lives, especially for children. Michael's mission for the Foundation isn't merely about getting more kids interested in swimming, but rather to use swimming as a means to improve children's lives in a number of ways.

For instance, one of the biggest barriers to swimming is a fear of water. One of the ways Michael got over his fear and built inner confidence, and now something that his Foundation offers, is a water safety course. The course is aimed at both children and their parents, with the additional aim of reducing the number of preventative drownings. On top of building confidence, the MPF uses swimming to provide children with mental health therapy, socialization through group activities, and lessons on how to achieve their goals, all through a strategic partnership with Special Olympics International and the Boys and Girls Club of America. The MPF is Michael's innovative way of continuing Debbie's commitment to education and finding his own joy in helping children grow.

Debbie's individual impact has also expanded. Drawing on her decades of experience as an educator, she now leads the charge as head of the Education Foundation for Baltimore County Public Schools. Like the time she went against conventional wisdom and convinced Michael's teachers that he'd be better off sitting at the back of the class, Debbie now persuades anyone who believes in education to contribute and help her solve the problem of how to provide schools with additional resources beyond their regular budgets. If anyone can find ways to improve the lives of over 106,000 students in Baltimore County, it's Debbie.

Being the Mother, Not the Coach

Debbie Phelps raised the most decorated Olympian of all time. That was never her end goal, however. She never pressured Michael, never burdened him with expectations, and never tracked his lap times. Her job was to be his mother; to be the role model he mirrored in stressful situations, and to give him support when he needed it.

Now parallel Michael's journey to greatness with the story of another sporting champion, who once said, "Being pushy is the worst thing a parent can be—if you push your children, you stop them enjoying whatever it is they're good at" (Moorhead, 2017).

Sir Andy Murray spent around 41 weeks as the number one tennis player in the world and bagged three Grand Slam titles over his career. Tennis most definitely ran through this legend's veins, with his maternal grandmother being a coach and his mother a champion in her own right before she turned to coaching and helped Andy and his older brother perfect their skills.

Judy was 10 years old when her mother, a volunteer tennis coach at a local club, taught her how to play tennis, a move that would ultimately lead to both of Judy's sons winning a Wimbledon title. In the 1970s, she played professional tennis and won a total of 64 junior and senior titles.

When Judy was 21, she married William Murray. Six years later, Judy gave birth to their first son, Jamie, with their second son, Andy, following a year later. Like Michael, Andy was nine years old when his parents split. Their divorce was finalized in 2005. During an interview, Andy blamed irreconcilable differences as the cause for their split. He explained that his parents never speak to each other or get along with one another (Wilson, 2023).

They almost lost their sons when a shooting took place at their school, known as the Dunblane massacre. A total of 16 children as well as their teacher were killed when gunman Thomas Hamilton stormed into the school's gymnasium with four handguns. During an interview, Judy gave harrowing details on the event. She explained that Andy's class was on their way to the gym for their next class when the shooting took place. The children were escorted to the headmaster's study where they had to sit and hide below the window. By the time it was safe for the children to go home, they still had no idea of what was happening.

Judy was working at the local toy shop when she heard about the shooting. Without giving her boss or coworkers any explanation, Judy grabbed her keys and drove off to school, thinking all the way that she might never see her children again. "There were too many cars on the road—everyone was trying to get there. I got angry, shouting 'Get out of the way!' About a quarter of a mile away I just got out and ran" (McRae, 2014).

The trio later settled in Glasgow, which was a challenging move for Judy as she was suddenly removed from everything and everyone she ever knew. Judy explains that since she felt so cut off from her own life, adjusting to her new reality was very difficult.

Not working at the time, Judy often felt stuck at home with her two sons and the chaos that motherhood can bring. She also didn't have a car at the time and was desperate for an escape. "I wanted something to get me out of the house because my kids were driving me nuts," Judy said (Gaur, 2023). It's a shame she hadn't heard of "Debbie Time."

In searching for a respite, Judy did a lot of soul-searching and reflection on what she could do well. Her thoughts immediately went to her own mother and how she volunteered as a tennis coach, so Judy decided to give it a try. This propelled her to not only find a way of escaping her daily challenges but also gave her a new career and source of income to care for her young sons. When Andy and Jamie showed interest in tennis, she became their first coach, teaching them the basics and later supporting them as they entered the big stage.

Andy's competitive nature showed from a very young age. When they played a board game together as a family, all hell would break loose if he didn't win. "He'd be the one who would tip the board up and strop and sulk," Judy said (Ferguson, 2015). She believes his highly competitive streak came from having an older brother, who due to having an extra year to grow and develop, was naturally better than him in many things. However, Andy was adamant in wanting to do whatever he could to beat Jamie, particularly in tennis.

This is also why she was so relieved when Andy won the Wimbledon tournament in 2013. As happy as Judy was for her son achieving the ultimate success as a tennis player, she also didn't have to deal with the same level of devastation he experienced just the year before when he lost out on the win. "It takes a lot to bring somebody back from that kind of low... I found the whole thing very, very stressful," Judy explained (Ferguson, 2015).

Since she started coaching her sons at a young age, she had to find the balance between pushing them on the tennis court and supporting them as their mother. Judy was always a very loving person, and from playing a lot with her children, she formed a close bond with them. As a result, she became her sons' first point of call whenever something went wrong or a big decision had to be made.

Because Judy grew up in a sporty household, she wanted the same for her own children. However, with famously wet Scottish weather not always allowing outdoor sports to take place, Judy had to become inventive in how she not only kept her sons busy but also honed their sporting talents and basic coordination skills. She started to invent games they could play indoors. But, because money was tight, they had to use things that were already lying around the house. For example, old cereal boxes would serve as a table tennis net across a table, with the lids from biscuit tins as their bats. They would move this to the floor and play with their hands when Judy needed the table. This gave them the wonderful ability to develop even more muscles as they couldn't rely on their legs to bring them closer to the ball.

Out of all the roles Judy has played in her life, motherhood remains her favorite one. "I love being a mother. I've got two great kids who are amazing–and great fun," she said (Ferguson, 2015). Her philosophy in life, which she always tried to teach them, was to aim high while keeping their feet firmly on the ground. "Don't be afraid to dream... but never forget where you came from, and always remain humble," she would tell them (Ferguson, 2015).

Judy not only taught her children how to play tennis but also about resilience and the importance of dealing with your emotions, on and off the court. This was put to the test when she was sexually assaulted during a function of an educational organization where she was the guest speaker. Judy recalled how a drunk man touched her inappropriately. It was toward the end of the meal that he came to sit next to Judy. She could tell that this man had too much to drink. He put his hand on her knee, which she removed. Next, he put his hand down the back of Judy's pants. Judy says she immediately got up and went to the bathroom, where she remained until it was time for her to deliver her speech. "I wanted to throw up. I was totally disgusted and didn't know what to do. It rocked me so badly." (Foster, 2022).

Judy's strength in getting out of that bathroom and standing in front of a room full of people to deliver her speech firmly places her in the category of a maternal maverick. Just like she didn't allow that man to take anything from her on the night, she didn't allow the challenges they faced to affect her children in a negative way. Instead, she raised two equally strong men, like Debbie did with Michael, who all took on the world and won.

Chapter 13:

Patricia Noah

My mom raised me as if there were no limitations on where I could go or what I could do. When I look back I realize she raised me like a white kid—not white culturally, but in the sense of believing that the world was my oyster, that I should speak up for myself, that my ideas and thoughts and decisions mattered.

Trevor Noah

The Survivor of Adversities

Known for his sharp wit and insightful commentary on global affairs, this Emmy award-winning comedian, talk show host, four-time GRAMMYs master of ceremonies, and best-selling author entertains audiences all over the world with his unique brand of comedy. When it was first announced he was taking over at the helm of America's beloved late-night satirical show *The Daily Show*, the news was met with a resounding "who?" But Trevor Noah quickly proved his mettle and brought a fresh, international voice to the show, tackling world events with a unique blend of humor and insightful storytelling. He even filmed the show from his home during the pandemic, making sure it remained relative and popular during those crazy times. He left *The Daily Show* after seven years, but he still engages with audiences regularly through his popular weekly podcast and other appearances.

Trevor grew up as a "white" child in a black family in a country where white and black people weren't allowed to mix at all. His parents weren't permitted to be friends, let alone have an intimate relationship. Yet, he isn't shy to admit that his conception and very being were considered to be a crime in South Africa, his country of birth. In fact, it was the title of his New York Times bestselling book, *Born a Crime*.

His mother, Patricia, gave him everything she didn't have as a child, which included not allowing racial discrimination get the better of them. She did so by combining a strict parenting style with the ability to see the humor in any situation they might find themselves in. This created the platform for Trevor to become a well-respected comedian, not just in South Africa but worldwide. Patricia's boldness in nurturing Trevor's identity outside societal constraints played a pivotal role in shaping the man he would become.

Even though he often makes fun of himself and his childhood on TV and when performing his sold-out comedy shows around the world, he has nothing but the utmost respect for his mother, whom he openly calls the hero in the story of his life. Patricia has been through incredible hardships in her life, which included having to seek advice from prostitutes on how to find accommodation and navigate her way around a new city to surviving Apartheid and being shot in the head by her former husband.

Patricia Noah's Journey and Influence

Patricia was born in 1964 in Johannesburg, South Africa. Growing up, she experienced a sense of not fitting in, clashing with her mother's expectations. At nine, she asked to live with her father, who initially agreed but then sent her to live with her aunt in Transkei. Stranded there for 12 years, she shared a small hut with 14 cousins from troubled families. In Transkei, a region with scarce resources, living conditions were dire yet Patricia was expected to help with farming. She often struggled to find enough food and had to compete with others for even the smallest scraps. She sometimes resorted to taking leftovers from animals or eating dirt to quell her hunger.

Despite her dire circumstances in Transkei, Patricia enjoyed going to the local missionary school where she learned to read and write in English. Eventually, she found a job at a nearby factory. The job gave her two things she cherished: A sense of independence and a daily meal.

Patricia's life improved further when she enrolled in a secretarial school at the age of 21. A year later, she decided to move to Johannesburg to escape the burden she termed the "black tax"—the pressure felt by impoverished Black people to uplift their families from the historic degradation they faced.

Patricia lived in a time when Apartheid was rife in her country and racial segregation and tension meant non-white people weren't allowed many of the basic human rights and other benefits that white people enjoyed. At one point, the apartheid government eased labor regulations in response to international pressure. It was little more than a token gesture, but it allowed Patricia to get secretarial work in a pharmaceutical company. However, her life outside of work was still a daily struggle.

At first, she slept in public bathrooms. Later, she connected with a group of Xhosa sex workers who taught her how to survive in the city. These women helped Patricia pretend to be a maid to move around without being noticed. Black maids in the city were required to carry official papers proving their work status and right to enter white areas for work; a perk other Black workers like secretaries didn't qualify for. But Patricia didn't have this documentation and was often arrested. She always managed to pay the fine with the money she had, and after being released from jail, she simply went back to being a "maid".

Friendships and especially sexual relationships between people from different racial groups were regarded as illegal during apartheid. But because Patricia lived in an artistically vibrant and progressive community that attracted whites who were either against or indifferent to apartheid, she befriended many whites. Among them was Robert, a Swiss-German who was much older than Patricia; their connection was more of a friendship than a romantic relationship.

One night Patricia asked Robert if he would be willing to start a family. She was set on having a baby without the pressures of marriage, but Robert wasn't keen on the idea. Since it was against the law, he would have no legal ties to the child. He eventually agreed.

Patricia gave birth to Trevor in 1984, 10 years before Apartheid in the country officially ended. In his memoir book *Born a Crime*, Trevor wrote that when his mother gave birth to a mixed-race baby who violated many rules in their country, she essentially gave birth to a crime (Weaver, 2023). To conceal her crime, Patricia told doctors that Trevor's father was of a different nationality. Since they had to comply with the official paperwork, the doctors listed Noah's father as unknown and nationality as "another country".

She also sent her son to colored daycare, as being colored is considered an official race in South Africa, and at times pretended to be her son's nanny when people questioned the differences in their skin color. Although the law prohibited them from having any contact, Patricia tried to sneak her young son to visit his father as often as they could. Her defiance against apartheid's oppressive laws by forming a bond with Trevor's father set a precedent of courage and love against all odds.

Eventually, Robert relocated to Cape Town and Patricia got married to a mechanic, Abel. The couple had two sons together. Unfortunately, Abel was a heavy drinker and when he was on a drunken binge, he would become violently abusive, particularly toward Patricia and Trevor. Trevor was a constant reminder that Patricia had a life and sexual relationship before Abel became part of their lives, and he struggled to come to terms with that. Trevor's light skin tone made this even worse and more difficult for Abel to deal with, as Trevor's existence was proof of Patricia breaking their country's laws.

Eventually, Patricia separated from Abel. Abel didn't take this well at all and, during a severe incident of domestic abuse after Patricia remarried, he shot Patricia twice, in her head and buttocks. Afterwards, he tried to hunt down Noah. He pleaded guilty to a charge of attempted murder and was sentenced to just three years of correctional service.

Patricia worked hard to provide for her young family, doing anything from bookkeeping to owning her own shop.

Finding the Humor Together

From an early age, Patricia and Trevor used humor to cope with their challenges. This exposed Trevor to different forms of humor that he still uses in his career and helped him develop a thick skin by constantly making fun of himself, his upbringing, and even his maternal culture. This was one of the biggest driving forces in the early comedic shows he did in South Africa before relocating to America.

In his book, Trevor tells the story of a comedic moment he shared with his mother while doing grocery shopping as a young child. He desperately wanted a toffee apple, so Patricia told him to grab one and meet her at the checkout line. When he returned, he told the cashier his mother, who was standing next to him, would pay for it. Since their skin colors are different, the cashier didn't make the connection between them. Patricia pretended not to know Trevor, so she paid for her groceries and left. Trevor ran after her in tears but when they met at the car, and he saw how his mother was laughing at this prank, he couldn't help but see the humor.

Patricia adopted a strict parenting style, which included giving him a hiding. She did so out of a deep desire to protect him from the challenging environment they lived in. She told her son that the reason why she was so strict with her young son was because she wanted the very best for him. She acted out of love, especially when she disciplined young Trevor. "If I don't punish you, the world will punish you even worse… the police don't love you. When I beat you, I'm trying to save you. When they beat you, they're trying to kill you," she used to tell Trevor (Weaver, 2023).

Even though they lived impoverished, Trevor never felt poor, as Patricia gave him many life experiences, with one of his best memories being having homemade sandwiches on picnics. They might've lived in a racially charged country where the government openly discriminated against people of color, yet she raised Trevor in a manner so that he didn't see race when he looked at others or himself.

Trevor explains that although he understood that people had different skin tones, he didn't associate black, brown, and white with skin, but with chocolate. In his family, he was milk chocolate, his mother dark chocolate, and his dad white chocolate. "My mother never referred to my dad as white or to me as mixed. So, when the other kids in Soweto called me 'white,' I just thought they had their colors mixed up, like they hadn't learned them properly," Trevor joked in his book (Weaver, 2023).

This again shows how effective Patricia was in protecting her son from the environment in which they lived. She also did everything she could to expose him to a life she didn't have when she was growing up. This included giving Trevor books she couldn't read and sending him to the types of schools she could only wish to go to. The vast difference between his family home and the life that Patricia gave her son helped him change his view of the world. Most of all, Patricia taught Trevor what true love is. "Love is a creative act. When you love someone you create a new world for them. My mother did that for me" (Weaver, 2023).

Trevor refers to his mother as the hero of his life story. He says that even though he always thought he would be the hero of his own story, now he very well understands that it's all his mother. "I was lucky enough to be in the shadow of a giant. My mom's magic dust sprinkled on me and I hope I have enough of it to be as brave as she was and continues to be," he said (Weaver, 2023).

The Ripple Effect of Patricia's Influence on Trevor Noah's Success

Born into a world where his very existence was a crime and constant challenge, Noah's journey from the poverty-stricken streets of Johannesburg to becoming a global icon is nothing short of remarkable. It would be so easy for him to be vengeful at the world given the horrors he and his mother had to live through. Think of the hatred you'd feel towards the person who shot your mother. Or imagine your mom pushing you out of a minibus in the middle of the night, and the two of you having to sprint away from the bus driver who's trying to kill you. Once they reached a safe place, however, the pair started laughing.

You see, Patricia Noah taught her son compassion and understanding. He refuses to carry the burden of hatred. Instead, he learned from her the importance of humility and finding humor in all of life's experiences. Her own story is one of relentless optimism. She constantly looked for ways to improve her station in life, with one of the most important ways being education. Education opened doors for her even when society had them firmly locked. She then invested all she could in her children's education, making sure they had more opportunities in their lives.

Trevor has taken up the torch from Patricia, investing in the education and career opportunities of children and youths in South Africa through the Trevor Noah Foundation. A major part of the Foundation's mission is to improve access to education and employment opportunities in the forgotten townships and underserved rural communities that millions of Black South Africans live in following decades of Apartheid.

While he sees Patricia as the hero of his story, he views learning as the greatest gift he has ever received, and he's paying it forward to the next generation.

Overcoming Trauma with Determined Optimism

Patricia demonstrated a unique blend of strict parenting alongside profound love and support. She disciplined Trevor not just for the sake of discipline but to prepare him for a world that might not always be kind or fair. She used humor as a coping mechanism and to keep their spirits up. By laughing together, Patricia taught Trevor not to let life weigh you down despite the constant absurdities and severe injustices they faced.

Patricia raised Trevor with the belief that he was not limited by the color of his skin or what society told them he could or couldn't do. She gave Trevor books to read, sent him to good schools, and exposed him to different experiences, showing him a world of possibilities if he dared to go for them.

And in the end, it was a dare that got him into comedy. He accepted a challenge by his friends to perform on a vacant comedy club stage. The crowd loved it. Trevor had always loved making people laugh but his performance in the club that night made him realize a passion for comedy that now drives his life.

The incredible story of Patricia having to fight, run, or study to save her child's life and get to a place where Trevor could live out his passions is in some ways similar to the story of a famous compatriot and her mother from the other side of the race divide.

Raised on her parents' farm in South Africa, Charlize Theron experienced significant challenges during her childhood, including the daily trauma and emotional distress of living with her alcoholic father, Charles.

Charlize recognized her passions early on. She convinced her mom, Gerda, that moving away to attend a boarding school that specialized in the arts was the right move for her if she wanted it to become a career. She was just 13 at the time.

During a visit from school in 1991, the turbulent situation at home took a horrific turn. In a drunken rage, Charles threatened both Gerda and 15-year-old Charlize with a shotgun, and actually shot at them three times, with all of the bullets luckily missing the frightened pair. Fearing for their lives, Gerda made the split-second decision to shoot her husband in self-defense, ending his life. The incident was ruled as such by authorities, given the clear threat they faced.

While the traumatic loss of her father shook Charlize's world, her mother's brave actions that night ultimately saved both their lives. And it was Gerda's unwavering support and encouragement in the years after the tragedy that helped Charlize get through this harrowing experience and empowered her to continue pursuing her dreams. "Her philosophy was: This is horrible. Acknowledge that this is horrible." said Charlize about her mother's hard-hitting guidance. "Now make a choice. Will this define you? Are you going to sink or are you going to swim?" (Marquina, 2017).

Despite their extremely modest means and the burdens of being a widowed single mother, Gerda worked tirelessly to provide Charlize with opportunities.

At age 16 Theron moved with her mother to Milan to work as a model. About a year later she settled in New York City, where she continued to model and began studying at the Joffrey Ballet School. A knee injury ended her chances of a career in dance, however, and she became depressed with her situation. Once again, Gerda came to Charlize's rescue. She brought her daughter out of her slump and bought her a one-way ticket to Los Angeles to go fulfill her destiny as a star.

One day, while at a Hollywood Boulevard bank, she tried to cash a few checks, including one from her mother to help with rent, which the bank rejected. Impressed with her performance while arguing and pleading with the bank teller, talent agent John Crosby, who was next in line, cashed the check for her and gave her his business card and soon after, her big break into the movie industry.

It was Gerda's continuous encouragement and belief in her daughter's potential that helped Charlize navigate the traumas of her youth and challenges of "making it", ultimately leading her to a successful career in Hollywood. And like Trevor, she was able to use her influence to make a real difference in people's lives.

Charlize founded the Charlize Theron Africa Outreach Project (CTAOP) in 2007. This project is dedicated to helping African youth stay safe from HIV and fighting against violence towards women. As a UN Messenger of Peace, Charlize channels the lessons from her personal journey, including the strength she witnessed in her mom on that fateful night, into efforts that make a meaningful impact.

Patricia and Gerda instilled in their children the values of perseverance and courage, giving them the best possible chance at becoming successful in their chosen professions. But they didn't stop there. Their success as individuals is further defined by their passionate advocacy for education and social justice. The strength and guidance provided by both mothers have left indelible marks on Trevor and Charlize's lives, allowing them to become the best in what they do, whether it's making people laugh, shooting a blockbuster film, or drawing attention to important issues in Africa.

Chapter 14:

Ata Johnson

I always say, if you got a good mom then you got a shot at becoming a good, caring human being.

Dwayne "The Rock" Johnson

The Angel in Human Form

He's known as the WWE pro-wrestling superstar turned bankable actor of big action blockbusters like *The Scorpion King, Black Adam, Jumanji,* and the *Fast & Furious* franchise. He can demand millions for a starring role thanks to the formidable presence he brought from the wrestling ring to the silver screen. He also lends his comedic talents to animated movies, where he isn't afraid to use his singing voice to entertain his audiences. But, before he reached these levels of success, Dwayne "The Rock" Johnson was simply the son of Ata Johnson, an amazing woman who her son believes is an angel in human form.

Ata went through big hardships in life, which included surviving lung cancer, severe poverty, a suicide attempt, and two serious car accidents. Yet, she still managed to teach her son about resilience and treating others in a way that he would treat her. Had it not been for her influence on Dwayne's life, he most likely wouldn't be known today as one of the nicest people in Hollywood.

Ata Johnson's Journey and Influence

Born in 1948 in Hawaii, Ata Johnson grew up in a family of wrestlers. Her adoptive father was a Samoan wrestler who also promoted the National Wrestling Alliance on the island. Her mother was also a wrestling promoter. She had two siblings, Toa and Peter. Peter was also involved in the sport and was the tag team partner of Rocky Johnson, who would later become Ata's husband. The family relocated to the United States in the 1970s.

Before Rocky married Ata, he was married to his first wife, Una Sparks. This didn't stop the development of a secret relationship between Rocky and Ata. Dwayne spoke out about his grandparents' reaction when they found out about the affair. Dwayne's grandparents didn't approve of the affair and forbade Ata from seeing Rocky. They were heartbroken but Ata realized that the only way her parents would stop objecting to their relationship was if she got pregnant, which she did. "I was born. And I became 'the glue' of the family," Dwayne said—he was six years old when his father got divorced and married Ata. The couple divorced in 2003 and Rocky died in 2020 from a pulmonary embolism (Dodd, 2023).

Growing up surrounded by wrestlers, Ata naturally found a career in the industry, appearing on many episodes of *WWE Raw* and *WrestleMania 2000*, to name just a couple.

Dwayne was a young boy when Rocky started coaching him in the wrestling ring. At the time, Dwayne didn't like the sport at all but is now grateful for the opportunities his parents gave him. "I was 13 and [he'd] say 'If you're gonna throw up, go outside. And if you're gonna cry, then go home to your mother.' I hated it then, but I embrace it now," he said (Dodd, 2023).

Initially, Dwayne wanted to create a career in American football, but a shoulder injury forced him to quit the sport. He then went back to his family heritage to follow in the footsteps of many of his family members in the wrestling ring. Known as The Rock, named after his father Rocky, Dwayne quickly gained popularity, which ultimately led him to his acting career in Hollywood.

The Sign of True Strength

Dwayne is known for being one of the physically strongest actors in Hollywood. He stands six feet, four inches tall and his 260 pounds body weight is filled with muscle. However, when asked, Dwayne is quick to say that his mother is his true source of strength, having overcome many hardships in her life. Ata's journey through adversity fortified her spirit and laid the foundation for Dwayne's understanding of true strength—rooted not in muscle, but in mettle and mercy.

Within a decade of tying the knot, her marriage was in trouble. In 1987, Rocky was blacklisted from wrestling after getting into trouble with the law, which led to his arrest as well as alcohol abuse. His drinking resulted in the couple facing severe financial difficulties, causing them to often move around to find a new, affordable place to live. However, despite the hardships they faced, Ata worked vigorously to provide for her family.

She also wouldn't allow these challenging times to get the better of Dwayne and always reminded him to look within to find the strength to carry on. When Dwayne eventually made it big, he bought his parents their first house in 1999. "Since then I always made sure my mom and dad have everything they'll ever need," he said (Dodd, 2023). Over the years, Dwayne bought his parents several houses.

When Dwayne was only 15 years old, the family lost their car due to an unpaid debt and faced eviction from their rental apartment. In that moment, life became too much for Ata to handle. One of Dwayne's first heroic acts followed; saving his mother's life when she tried to commit suicide.

When Ata and Dwayne were driving on Interstate 65 in Nashville, Ata suddenly and without warning stopped the car, got out, and walked straight into oncoming traffic. Dwayne ran to his mother and pulled her back to the gravel on the side of the road. "What's crazy about that suicide attempt is to this day, she has no recollection of it whatsoever. Probably best she doesn't," he said in an interview (Kubota, 2023). This pivotal experience, though harrowing, taught Dwayne to value life and to live every day to the fullest.

Unfortunately, her new-death experience on the highway wasn't the only time Dwayne came close to saying goodbye to his beloved mother. In 2009, Ata was diagnosed with stage three lung cancer and underwent rigorous treatment. A year later, her body was free from cancer. During an interview, Dwayne said, "This past summer my mom was diagnosed with stage three lung cancer. She fought. She had chemotherapy, radiation. She fought like a warrior. And I'm happy to tell you, she is cancer-free" (RandyW, 2010). The way she fought her cancer showed her son that he should never give up, no matter how bleak the situation might seem.

Five years later, Ata and Dwayne's cousin were in a head-on accident caused by a drunk driver. In a post on Instagram, Dwayne admitted that his first thought was to find the driver responsible for the accident and get revenge. After he had time to calm down, reflect on what happened, and think about the bigger picture, he decided against making the situation worse. He said, "But then you realize the most important thing is my family lived through this and we can hug each other that much tighter these days. Hug your own family tighter today and be grateful you can tell them you love them" (David, 2023).

The trials of life, from the perils of accidents to the tests of character, strengthened his bond with Ata, and reminded him of what truly matters. And in sharing these stories, Dwayne invites us to reflect on our own relationships, to cherish and honor those bonds that shape us, urging us to hold our loved ones close.

Nine years later, she was hospitalized in another serious car accident, which she luckily survived. Again, Dwayne posted on Instagram about it, "This woman has survived lung cancer, tough marriage, head on collision with a drunk driver, and attempted suicide. She's a survivor, in ways that make angels and miracles real" (David, 2023). After these two accidents, Dwayne has repeatedly urged people to value their mothers and fathers and the role they play in our lives, just like he values Ata every day, especially after he already lost his dad.

Dwayne is a self-confessed mommy's boy who often sings Ata's praises. He openly refers to her as his matriarch, and on her 74th birthday, he wrote about her on his Instagram page, "We get such joy seeing you radiate and smile and proudly display our culture. Grace, beauty, dignity, respect and strength. You can feel the mana of our ancestors all around us" (David, 2023).

Dwayne is clearly never too shy to give compliments to his mother, it just adds to his persona as a big softy. But he also showers her with gifts and treats. He aims to make sure that he does everything he can to make sure his mother is happy and thriving. During his childhood, she taught him what true love, compassion, and care really means. Now, Dwayne goes out of his way to give her the life she has always deserved. "When

I was a little boy, I hated when my mom would cry. These days, I'll happily take her tears of joy" (Camargo, 2022).

The Ripple Effect of Ata's Influence on Dwayne Johnson's Success

Known as a true gentleman and one of the nicest people in Hollywood, Dwayne credits his mother for shaping the person he is today. He recalls one of the best pieces of advice his mother gave him when he was still young, "My mom would always tell me, 'Listen, you can see whomever you want. But always, always, always treat them nice like you would treat me. Always'" (Nath, 2022).

Ata's advice has always stayed close to Dwayne's heart even as he closes in on becoming a billionaire. It would be so easy for him to give millions to charity without truly caring about who he's helping and why. But her words are so much a part of who he is that he can't help but do all he can for each noble cause.

For example, since making it big in the WWE, Dwayne has been an active supporter in children's health initiatives, including the Make-A-Wish Foundation, the well-known nonprofit organization that fulfills the wishes of children with terminal and life-threatening medical conditions. He has always made time to meet his young fans, often surprising them at an event or at their hospital bed. Apart from a big hug, a common wish is singing them his song from *Moana*, which he is more than happy to grant. His involvement in supporting pediatric healthcare extends beyond meeting young fans; he also helps families raise money for their children's medical bills.

Other causes Dwayne gives financial aid to and raises awareness of include education, military veterans, and disaster relief efforts. When members of the Screen Actors Guild - American Federation of

Television and Radio Artists (SAG-AFTRA) went on strike, he made a seven-figure donation that meant thousands of unpaid actors could keep a roof over their children's heads and food on the table. He even once donated the remaining balance needed to perform life-saving surgery on an abandoned puppy. Basically, he'll get involved in any charitable endeavor that lets him make a positive difference in people's lives. What's more, others with the means to give see his generosity and want to step up and join him.

Being the Rock that Moves Mars

There's another superstar with Hawaiian roots whose success was sculpted through his family's legacy and the tight bond with his loving mother. This Grammy award-winning singer has the amazing ability to combine the charm of retro sounds and contemporary notes with a dazzling stage presence that rivals The Rock to make him loved by fans young and old.

Bruno Mars' music has defined a generation. His infectious chart-topping melodies effortlessly blend the old with the new. From epic love ballads *Just the Way You Are*, *Marry You* and *Locked Out of Heaven* to party anthems *Uptown Funk* and *24K Magic*, his songs are the soundtrack to countless celebrations and memorable moments.

It comes as no surprise that the man who rose to fame due to his magical singing voice, catchy tunes, and energetic dance moves actually grew up in a very musical family that would constantly sing and dance together. As a youngster, he made a name for himself impersonating Elvis Presley. And he wrote his first song when he was only four years old, dedicating it to his mother, Bernadette Hernandez, who helped cultivate his musical and dancing talents and was his biggest supporter until the day of her sudden death in 2013 aged just 55.

Born in the Philippines in 1957, Bernadette was part of a big family with six brothers. Her father was the only breadwinner in the family and

Bernadette's mother got worried over how they would support everyone's needs. To help this young family, Bernadette's grandmother, an American citizen living in San Francisco, suggested some of her grandchildren should live with her, where she believed they might have better opportunities and a more stable upbringing.

Bernadette was 10 years old when they hopped onto a ship to travel from the Philippines to America. While en route, the ship had a stopover in Hawaii. This island reminded them so much of home that they decided to stay there and create a new life for their family. It was here that young Bernadette's dancing and musical talent was noticed. From very early on, Bernadette already displayed a natural affinity for rhythmic movement and a captivating stage presence. She became a singer and a hula dancer, enchanting local residents by the grace and energy she brought to her performances.

During one of her shows, she performed with a percussionist originally from New York of Puerto Rican and Jewish descent, Peter Hernandez. Their mutual love for music resulted in them falling in love. Soon after, they were married and had six children. They named their fourth child and second son Peter Gene Hernandez, who would grow up to become the world-famous musician, Bruno Mars.

The family didn't grow up rich. Instead, at one stage the Hernandez family was so poor that they stayed in a tiny apartment without a bathroom and often went days without having any electricity. This taught Bruno not to attach too much value to earthly possessions. "We had it all. We had each other," he was quoted as saying (Liwag Dixon & Ledford, 2023).

Bernadette eventually left Peter, and her children chose to stay with her. In 2013, she died unexpectedly from a brain aneurysm at the age of 55. This devastating loss left an indelible mark on Bruno and his siblings, who had already weathered so much adversity in their young lives.

Since his parents were both performers, Bruno basically grew up on stage and surrounded by music. Bernadette invested in her young son's music by buying him his first instrument, a little piano. Instead of banging the notes as you'd expect from such a young child, Bruno's musicality kicked in and he immediately started playing tunes.

He started his solo performance career when he was only four years old as an Elvis impersonator; the world's youngest, in fact. Bruno was once asked what he admired about Elvis enough to impersonate him in public and four-year-old Bruno replied that he admired his singing, his dancing, and his lips. It was also around that time he got the nickname Bruno, named after the wrestler Bruno Sammartino, whom he resembled (Tocino, 2016). During an interview with *Inquirer Lifestyle*, Bernadette said that Bruno was "singing even before he started talking" (Liwag Dixon & Ledford, 2023).

The family created their own band to perform together, where Bruno got the opportunity to perform his own song titled *I Love You Mom*, in which he sings about his "favorite girl." Some of the lyrics include, "My mommy helps me with my voice, cuz a superstar singer is my first choice. My parents help me out cuz I know they love me. I just wish they buy me more toys and candy." Bruno loved performing with his family (En & Carneiro, 2013).

When Bruno tried to get his own recording deals as an adult, he opted to use his nickname as a stage name. Initially, he planned to only use the one name, like his hero Elvis, but recording companies still compared him to Spanish singer Enrique Iglesias. To be more unique and avoid racial stereotyping based on his looks and surname, he added "Mars" to his name, which made him sound like he was from another planet (Tocino, 2016). Bruno's calculated rebranding allowed him to carve out his own distinct musical niche and avoid being pigeonholed as just another Latin pop artist.

For a long time, Bruno struggled to cope with his mother's death. He said that not only has his life changed forever, but he would trade his musical success to have her back. During an interview, he said that when the woman who taught you everything you know, including what love is, is no longer with you, a piece of you dies with her. "You just gotta know that she's with me everywhere I go. It shows you the real importance of life. Nothing else matters in this world but family and your loved ones," he said during an interview with *Latina* (Kimble, 2017).

Bruno paid a special tribute to her during his rousing Super Bowl XLVIII halftime show performance, with Bernadette's name written across his drum kit in tattoo-style lettering on a banner across a red love heart. He was so close to his beloved mom that he had her name tattooed on his shoulder for real.

Being such a close family and having the great experience of performing together is still important to Bruno and his siblings. In fact, his older brother Eric Hernandez left his job as a police officer to play the drums in Bruno's band.

Bernadette didn't just bring musical talent and the importance of family to her talented son, but she also taught Bruno to cook. He especially enjoys cooking traditional dishes from the Philippines, such as his favorite dish chicken adobo.

Like Dwayne, Bruno is quick to share some of his wealth to support global relief efforts, including The Rainforest Foundation, Red Cross, and Save the Children. He also made huge donations to victims of Typhoon Yolanda in the Philippines, Bernadette's homeland, and to the city of Flint, Michigan, in the wake of their ongoing water contamination crisis. From his stage, he can call upon tens of thousands of people to join him and stand together in support of people who desperately need it.

The admiration and affection Bruno and Dwayne hold for Bernadette and Ata illuminate the profound impact a mother's love, guidance, and strength can have on her child's journey through life. The lessons and values of both mothers live on through their sons as they continue to entertain and help millions around the world.

Chapter 15:

Adele Sandberg

My husband and I raised our three children—Sheryl, David, and Michelle—to believe that they could achieve any dream as long as they were willing to work hard.

Adele Sandberg

Resilience and Growth

How can a person be so highly sought after that they're personally invited to become a chief of staff in government? How can a person stand out among their peers, particularly as a woman in an industry that is largely run by men? How can a person navigate that environment while trying to turn a relatively new business into a highly profitable empire in only a few years? Only one woman holds the answers to all of these questions: Sheryl Sandberg.

After attending public school in Miami, Sheryl earned her MBA from Harvard Business School before entering the corporate world. However, when her former professor, Lawrence Summers, became the deputy Treasury secretary in the Bill Clinton administration, he recruited Sheryl as his chief of staff. She held this position until George Bush took over the presidency.

This was when Sheryl made her big move to the tech industry. She first started at Google, where she eventually became the vice president for Global Online Sales and Operations. At a Christmas party in 2007, Sheryl met Facebook founder Mark Zuckerberg. He was so impressed with her that he made it his mission to convince her to join his company. He met with her once or twice a week, either at a restaurant or Sheryl's home. Eventually, his persistence paid off and Sheryl became Facebook's chief operating officer. She stayed with Meta, Facebook's holding company, until June 2022, and remained the first woman on their board of directors for a further two years.

During this time, Sheryl also became a best-selling author, first penning *Lean In: Women, Work, and the Will to Lead*, published in 2013, and then *Option B: Facing Adversity, Building Resilience, and Finding Joy*, published in 2017. Her first book dealt primarily with the lack of women in business and leadership positions, while the second focused on dealing with grief, which came in response to the sudden death of her husband, Dave Goldberg, in 2015.

Regarded by many as one of the most influential women in business, Sheryl reached incredible success. But what sets her apart from other women who enter the business world? While there may have been many factors contributing to her drive and passion, Sheryl often gives recognition to her mother, Adele Sandberg, whom she regards as her number one role model.

Adele Sandberg's Journey and Influence

Adele Sandberg was born into an impoverished immigrant family who lived in a rundown building in Lower East Side, New York. As a young woman, Adele was told she had only two career choices: nursing or teaching. She qualified as an English teacher and married Joel Sandberg, an ophthalmologist. Despite the limited career options available for women during that time, Adele had big dreams for her future and studied toward obtaining her Ph.D. However, before finishing her doctorate, Adele became pregnant with Sheryl. She left her job and studies to raise her children.

Her grandmother played a major role in her upbringing, as she showed Adele that hard work and determination can change your life. During an interview with Sheryl for *Huffington Post*'s #TalkToMe series, Adele spoke about her grandmother. "We called her The Rock because she was so strong and steadfast and she worked hard all of her life" (Gebreyes, 2016).

Her grandmother also instilled the importance of reaching out to others, particularly the less fortunate. They had many small cans in their home where they would add coins to donate to charity. Even in months when their finances were tight, she would still give to others. She believed that their prayers for making it through the month would be answered if they always remembered to look after the less fortunate. Then, she would continue to add coins to the can.

Adele has made a name for herself by caring for others. She started the Ear Piece Foundation, which aims to educate young people on the dangers of noise-induced hearing damage and motivate them to take measures to protect their ears and hearing. With her husband, Adele also became involved in fighting for the rights of Soviet Jews who wanted to escape their living conditions.

Adele and Joel's dedication to others is a major source of inspiration for Sheryl. She has been quoted as saying that her parents are the perfect role models of what a true commitment to improving the world looks like and how much of an impact that can make in the lives of others.

Inspiring Change Despite Challenges

Sheryl is very vocal about her appreciation of her mother and the role Adele has played in her life and success. She's quoted as saying her mother has always been her biggest source of inspiration as she leads by example. This includes what hard work and dedication look like as well as finding joy and giving back to others. She does this in an optimistic way, always seeking out the positives in any challenging situation she might find herself in. "Mom, I could never thank you enough for being the person I most inspire to live up to in my life" (Garner, 2022).

The fact that Adele had to leave her job and studies to care for her children inspired Sheryl to continuously call for improvements in the rights of working women. She addresses this in her first book and posted about it on her own Facebook account. In a 2016 Mother's Day post, Sheryl lashed out about the lack of paid maternity and family leave for women in the United States. She believes that being a mother is not just the most important and humbling job ever, but also the most rewarding. This is why it's important that mothers, particularly single mothers, should be supported in every way possible. Sheryl's acknowledgment of her mother's influence sheds light on the importance of role models in shaping your approach to life and work, emphasizing the value of leading by example.

It is no surprise that Sheryl has also dedicated her 2013 book to her parents, "for raising me to believe that everything is possible" (United Hatzalah, 2021). In this book, Sheryl encourages women to pursue their dreams, whether it's at work or home. She explains that during her childhood, Adele did everything she could for her family. "So thank you, Mom, for inspiring me and encouraging me to lean in from my childhood until today. And thank you, Mom, for leaning in and making your children your life's work" (Samakow, 2013).

The Ripple Effect of Adele's Influence on Sheryl Sandberg's Success

Sheryl Sandberg's journey through her groundbreaking work at Google and Meta, and considering her role as a pioneering woman in the tech industry, offers a richer understanding of her legacy. At Google, Sheryl was instrumental in scaling the ad and sales team from four to 4,000 people, transforming Google's advertising business into a multibillion-dollar powerhouse. This set the stage for her monumental impact at Meta, where she significantly shaped the company's business strategy. Her strategic insight turned Facebook's vast user data into lucrative ad revenue, driving the company to profitability by 2010.

Sheryl's tenure at these tech giants shows just how good she is at navigating and leading within male-dominated spaces. She uses her deep knowledge of both technology and policy to steer these companies through rapid growth and numerous challenges. Her departure from Meta after 14 years marked the end of an era but it provided an opportunity to reflect on and highlight her lasting influence on the company and the tech industry at large. Sheryl's work, particularly her ability to merge technological innovation with business strategy, set new standards for how tech companies operate and compete on a global scale.

Furthermore, Sheryl's legacy is intertwined with her advocacy for women in the workplace. Despite mixed reactions to her book, her efforts to encourage women to pursue their ambitions and her candid discussions about the challenges women face in climbing the corporate ladder have sparked important conversations and inspired many.

In essence, Sheryl's contributions to Google and Meta, combined with her role as a female leader in tech, illustrate how she has been a transformative figure. Her work at these companies not only reshaped the digital landscape but also paved the way for future generations of women in technology, echoing the broader societal impact of her mother's influence on her.

Security and Growth from Humble Beginnings

Adele Sandberg's journey from an immigrant family to becoming a community leader shows the essence of American perseverance, setting a profound example for her children. Yet it's Adele's foundational belief in hard work acting as the key to achieving dreams that has clearly left a mark on Sheryl.

Anyone fortunate enough to cross paths with Sheryl walks away from their encounter inspired. There's another remarkable individual who has an equally profound impact on the people he meets. And like Sheryl, he came from a poor immigrant family to become one of the most popular and respected people in tech.

Gary Vaynerchuk arrived in America as a poor immigrant from Belarus with parents who couldn't understand or speak a word of English. Just imagine, you're a child in a strange country, you have no clue what the people there are saying, and you also can't afford any of the things the other kids around you take for granted. While those experiences can be absolutely traumatic for someone so young, he overcame the many obstacles he faced because. But as you'll see, Gary actually did have the things children need to feel secure and grow, things that help them become successful, independent people. In fact, Gary showed his entrepreneurial skill at the age of just six and grew his father's business into a multimillion-dollar enterprise when he was still a teenager.

Gary's journey to success wasn't a solitary one. Behind every step he took and every risk he embraced was a steadfast presence. While he was growing through the ranks, his mother, Tamara Vaynerchuk was there with him, supporting him through all his ventures and providing "rainbows" where others might have been blinded by their poverty mindset and given up. Her unwavering support as she navigated her family through life's challenges illuminates the profound impact of maternal love and guidance on a child's path to success.

Tamara Vaynerchuk's early life in Belarus underpins a tale of loss, resilience, and hope, setting the stage for a life of impactful teachings and survival. Tamara was born in the late 1950s in Belarus, part of the former Soviet Union, a place Gary refers to as an "extremely unhappy place back then as it was facing enormous cultural and political issues" (Vaynerchuk, 2016). Many of their family members were killed during unrest in the country, including Tamara's mother, whom she lost when she was only five years old. Her grandmother raised her.

She married Sasha Vaynerchuk when she was young and gave birth to Gary when she was 20 years old. They moved to America with Sasha's family, a country she didn't know and where she was expected to speak a language she didn't understand.

Shortly after arriving, she had another baby, a daughter named Liz, and then later another son named AJ. Tamara had to stay home to raise her young children while Sasha was working 15-hour shifts to try to provide for his family.

By the time Tamara turned 25, she had had to deal with more adversity than most people would in their entire lives. The way that she takes all these challenges in her stride is one of the many things that Gary admires about his mother. "She faces it all without a complaint. That's how incredible she is," Gary wrote in a blog about his mother (Vaynerchuk, 2016).

Even at that young age, she had a wealth of knowledge, particularly emotional intelligence and empathy, and wasn't scared of taking risks for her young children. Gary refers to her as the "emotional bedrock" of her family. He explains that his mother is one of the most empathetic people he knows, with high levels of self-awareness and gratitude for everything and everyone she has in her life. "She was able to map and reverse-engineer all of her children. Even though each of us had very different personalities and needs, she was able to figure out the best for each of us" (Vaynerchuk, 2016). Her approach to motherhood, characterized by empathy and a deep understanding of her children, showcases the profound influence mothers like Tamara and Adele have in fostering their children's individual paths to success.

The humble beginnings of the Sandbergs and the Vaynerchuks in America highlight the stark realities faced by many immigrant families, emphasizing the value of contentment and love over material wealth. When the Vaynerchuk family came to America, they were "ridiculously poor." Gary has indicated that even though he didn't have many of the things other children had, he knew happiness and love. "My mom made it awesome... I did not have all these pressures that gave me all this gray hair. I was a kid and I had the best mom of all time, and everything was rainbows," Gary says (Jones, 2023). He believes the main reason why he easily found happiness in life is because he was raised being happy with very little. He says there are too many people living in big houses with lots of money who can't find true happiness in their lives.

While his mother stayed at home to raise their children, Gary's dad had to try to find work to support his family. When he started earning a constant income, Tamara encouraged her husband to save as much money as they could to improve their family's lives. "I lived with nine family members in a studio apartment," Gary says. His dad worked as a stock counter and rack packer at a local liquor store. He had bigger dreams for his family and wanted to give them the American Dream. So, he saved as much as he could, and eventually he bought his own liquor store. "A funny thing happens when you don't spend any money for four years. You actually accumulate it," Gary said (teamgaryvee, 2020).

Gary's entrepreneurial spirit started to shine through from a young age. With the help of his mother, he started selling baseball cards and lemonade in Edison, New Jersey. By the time he turned six, he ran seven lemonade stands. At the age of 12, he added selling baseball cards to his business acumen. "I was selling $1000 – $2000 worth of merchandise each weekend at the malls in New Jersey" (teamgaryvee, 2020).

Gary believes he learned some of his valuable lessons about business during this foundational stage of his life. When he was 14 years old, he started working part-time in his dad's liquor store. Seeing people buy and collect wine in the same way they would buy lemonade at the lemonade stands his mother helped him to run gave him new ideas on how to grow this business even more. This led him to develop the first-ever wine-centric e-commerce business in America. Over the next few years, he grew his father's business from a $3 million dollar company to a $60 million enterprise.

That was just the start of his business endeavors. Since then, he has become the CEO of the advertising company VaynerMedia, chairman of VaynerX, co-founder of VaynerSports, and bestselling author. He also made money investing in companies like Facebook, Snap, Venmo, and Twitter (now X), to name a few.

Gary openly attributes his success to his mother. The manner in which she raised him helps him to not get big-headed over his success. "It's not hard for me to stay grounded. My mother taught me how to believe in myself the most, while still allowing me to recognize the value in others," he says. She always supported her son and took on the role of the biggest cheerleader in his life. That's not to say he never faced any consequences when he misbehaved or did something wrong. Gary says Tamara provided him with the perfect mix of acknowledgment, support, and freedom while encouraging him to make the most of his strengths (Vaynerchuk, 2016).

He believes her only downfall in life is her shyness, but attributes that to feeling self-conscious about her accent. "I wish she wasn't so shy because she would provide enormous amounts of value to all of you as she did for me. If you think I provide any value, imagine what the person who built me is like," Gary wrote (Vaynerchuk, 2016).

Despite her eldest son's vast success, Tamara has chosen to stay out of the public eye, supporting her son from the side. Her shyness and self-consciousness about her accent aside, Tamara's immense value as a mother and influencer remains undeniable.

Tamara taught Gary invaluable lessons about life; to be empathetic, to maintain integrity, and to always remember where you come from, no matter how high you fly. These lessons have guided Gary in his business ventures and pushed him to use his platform to make a real difference in the world. Through initiatives and leadership roles, Gary has been able to extend his mother's teachings, creating ripples of positive change and inspiring others to give back to their communities. It's the kind of impact that truly defines success.

One of the primary platforms Gary leverages as a powerful tool to inspire and motivate his audience is podcasts. *The GaryVee Audio Experience* features a variety of episodes including #AskGaryVee show segments, keynote speeches, and interviews with other successful entrepreneurs and influencers—all providing a mix of practical business advice, personal development insights, and motivational content.

Listeners frequently express how Gary's podcasts have profoundly impacted their lives. For example, Ray Wood, the host of the *Top Agents Playbook* podcast, referred to Gary as his "marketing hero." He mentioned that he has implemented many of Gary's ideas with amazing results, highlighting Gary's significant influence on his career and personal development (Top Agents Playbook, 2016).

Gary also inspires individuals outside the business realm to reach new heights, often people with backgrounds similar to his own. For instance, Glorian, a 19-year-old immigrant from Venezuela, found motivation in Gary's story as a first-generation immigrant to pursue her dream of becoming a psychologist despite financial challenges. Inspired by Gary's emphasis on self-awareness and patience, and supported by a mother who values education (sound familiar?), she worked to save money for college and improve her English.

By consistently delivering content that addresses both the tactical and emotional aspects of entrepreneurship, Gary Vaynerchuk has established his podcasts as essential resources for aspiring entrepreneurs and business professionals seeking inspiration and actionable advice.

When leaders like Sheryl and Gary combine their professional achievements with personal passion and empathy, they inspire growth and positive change in the same way Adele and Tamara inspired them towards monumental success.

Chapter 16:

Sonya Carson

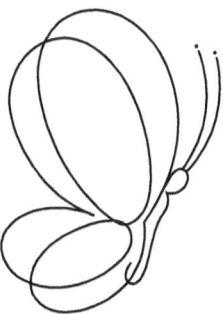

Over the years my mother's steadfast faith in God has inspired me, particularly when I had to perform extremely difficult surgical procedures.

Benjamin Carson M.D.

Believing in Success

His story transcends the boundary between science and service, leading him from the operating room to a major national political platform. He was the youngest chief of pediatric surgery in America and pioneered many intricate surgeries, from separating conjoined twins to performing neurosurgery on a fetus while still in the womb. After retiring from medicine, he turned his attention to politics, where he became the Secretary of Housing and Urban Development, and was even in the running to become the president of the United States. But the story of Dr. Ben Carson begins not with his own achievements, but with the foundation laid by a deeply spiritual upbringing, guided by his mother's unwavering faith.

Ben's mother, Sonya, was the driving force in his life. Even though she only had a third-grade level education and got married at the age of 13, she recognized the importance of reading and being educated for her children. Her story is a testament to the idea that the most profound impacts often stem from the humblest beginnings. Ben credits his success to his mother and her unquestionable belief in her sons and in God.

Sonya Carson's Journey and Influence

Sonya's early life was marked by hardship and struggle. Born in Tennessee in 1928, she grew up in a foster home and left school after only obtaining a grade three qualification. She was only 13 years old when she married Robert Carson, who at 28 was more than double her age. He was a minister at the church young Sonya attended. She believed that he was saving her from her impoverished living circumstances. Shortly after getting married, the couple moved to Detroit, where Sonya gave birth to two sons, first Curtis and, two years later, Ben. She was a devoted mother, and her sons were the center of her world.

When young Ben was only eight years old, Sonya discovered that her preacher-husband was actually a bigamist who had another secret family. Shortly after she made this discovery, Sonya divorced Robert. After briefly moving her sons to stay with her sister in Boston, she returned to Detroit where she worked three jobs to support her sons, one of which was as a domestic worker. At one point, Sonya became so depressed that she was hospitalized.

You'd think that her traumatic experience with her minister ex-husband would drive Sonya to view religion in a negative light, but she found refuge in her faith and remained a devout member of the Seventh Day Adventist Church. She prayed every time things might go wrong, which was the case when Ben brought home a bad report card in fifth grade, and she asked God to give her the wisdom she needed to assist her boys with their schoolwork. Drawing on the adversity of her life and the strength she found from God, Sonya crafted a vision of education and faith for her children that defied her own limited formal schooling.

From Bad Report to Surgeon Extraordinaire

Since she didn't have any formal education to speak of, she wanted better for her sons. Working in the homes of very successful and wealthy people, she saw those children were reading much more than they were playing or watching TV. She would often tell Ben, "Bennie, if you can read, honey, you can learn just about anything you want to know," (Denison, 2015). She encouraged learning by limiting their screen time to two shows per week on TV and would often take them to the public library. She expected them to read at least two library books per week, after which they had to write a report on one of these books. She would then pretend to grade their reports. The boys didn't realize until much later that Sonya couldn't actually read.

When she noticed Ben struggled to see, she emptied all her savings in her cookie jar to get him glasses. Whenever he would question himself or his own abilities, she would simply ask him, "Do you have a brain? Then you can think yourself out of that" (Dascher, 2018).

Sonya's intervention helped Ben excel at school to such an extent that he was able to attend Yale University. Later, he studied medicine at the University of Michigan and completed his residency at Johns Hopkins. Sonya never allowed their upbringing or race to get the better of her sons. "It doesn't matter what color you are. If you're good, you'll be recognized. Because people, even if they're prejudiced, are going to want the best. You just have to make being the best your goal in life," she taught them (Dascher, 2018). In the pivotal moments of Ben Carson's youth, Sonya's decisive actions against adversity set the stage for a story of unparalleled success.

An amazing career followed. He served as the Director of Pediatric Neurosurgery at Johns Hopkins from 1984 until he eventually retired in 2013, becoming the youngest chief of pediatric neurosurgery in America. In 1987 he became the first neurosurgeon to separate conjoined twins, and he pioneered a neurosurgical procedure on a fetus while still in the womb. He also developed new ways of managing seizures and received more than 60 honorary doctorate degrees.

After putting down his scrubs and scalpel, Ben turned his attention to politics and served as the Secretary of Housing and Urban Development from 2017 to 2021. In 2016, he was even in the running as a presidential candidate during the Republican primaries.

Sonya Carson's life serves as a profound reminder that the strength of a mother's faith and conviction can elevate her children to heights unimaginable. Sonya was such a big inspiration to Ben that he and his wife Candy founded The Carson Scholars Fund in 1994. This fund aimed at supporting two initiatives: The Carson Scholars Program that awards scholarships to students who achieve academic excellence, and The Ben Carson Reading Project, where children are invited to read. The Carson Scholars Fund and the Ben Carson Reading Project are but a few examples of how Sonya's legacy continues to inspire and uplift future generations.

They also created the Sonya Award, given to children who frequently attend the various reading rooms of the Ben Carson Reading Project. This award also serves to recognize various role models in the community, particularly those who share Sonya's drive and beliefs.

Sonya's life motto that she taught her sons is, "Learn to do your best and God will do the rest." This helped Ben to remain focused on what he wanted to achieve in his life. "I not only saw and felt the difference my mother made in my life, I am still living out that difference as a man" (Denison, 2015). Through Sonya's teachings, Ben learned to harness his faith and intellect in service of his dreams, embodying the principle that dedication and belief can overcome any obstacle.

Sonya passed away in 2017 at the age of 88. In celebrating her life, Ben wrote, "All that I am is because of the love of my mother. She was one of God's greatest blessings to me." He says it was her amazing foresight that helped him reach his dreams. Even though she had very limited education, she understood how success is achieved and did everything she could to make sure her children would be geared for greatness. "If anyone had a reason to make excuses, it was her, but she refused to be a victim and would not permit us to develop the victim mentality either" (Adventist Review Staff, 2017).

The Ripple Effect of Sonya's Influence on Ben Carson's Success

Sonya and Ben Carson are shining examples to the power of maternal influence, illustrating that the true essence of success is not measured merely by accolades or positions but by the depth of character and the impact a person can have on the world around them.

Think about the story of Sonya "grading" her son's book reports even though she couldn't read, never mind give any kind of specific feedback on the actual report. But it worked. Her sons actually cared about the books and reports, solidifying what they had read by creating detailed articles about each one. That's Sonya's incredible knack for ingenuity and resourcefulness on display. It was sort of like a placebo Ben might give a patient to improve their condition through the power of suggestion. And so, from her insistence on the transformative power of reading and education to her steadfast belief in the potential of her sons, it comes as no surprise that Sonya's principles are echoed throughout Ben's own literary contributions.

His most famous book, *Gifted Hands*, chronicles his journey from a struggling student in Detroit to a pioneering neurosurgeon and emphasizes the transformative power of education and reading. This autobiography has inspired many people by showing how determination and education can lead to exceptional achievements despite difficult circumstances. For instance, Ron Tullos, a medical student, was inspired to pursue a medical career after reading the book and meeting Ben Carson in person. Carson's message of education, determination, and hard work resonated with Tullos, who came from a disadvantaged background and was similarly raised by a mother who "was a very smart lady for not having a lot of education" (Woodard, 2014), and motivated him to overcome obstacles and strive for excellence in his education and career.

His other notable works include *Think Big* and *Take the Risk*. In *Think Big*, Ben extends Sonya's view on personal virtues and life philosophies that contribute to success, such as talent, honesty, and knowledge. This book serves as both a motivational guide and a practical approach to overcoming adversity with wisdom and integrity. *Take the Risk*, on the other hand, explores the concept of risk management in personal and professional contexts, providing insights into making confident choices amidst life's uncertainties.

Additionally, *America the Beautiful* and *One Nation* reflect his thoughts on American values and political ideologies, offering his perspective on what makes America unique and how its citizens can work towards a more unified and prosperous future. Reflecting on his upbringing and the profound influence of his mother, Ben discusses how personal responsibility, education, and moral integrity are crucial for national prosperity and unity. He argues that understanding America's past is essential to navigating its future, offering insights into the nation's capacity for renewal amidst challenges—pretty much the Carson formula for success.

New York Times bestselling author Ben Carson's books provide not just an account of his life and career, but also a roadmap for personal development and civic responsibility. These works continue to influence and inspire readers around the world, encouraging them to pursue excellence and engage thoughtfully with the challenges they face. Were it not for the book reports Sonya made him write, who knows if Ben would even have considered writing a book let alone several that have inspired millions.

Learning at Home and Making Books a Priority

The story of Ben and Sonya really shows how much of an impact a mother can have on her child's path to success. Sonya was simply amazing when it came to raising him and his brother. She had this exemplary approach to child rearing, blending firmness with love, setting high expectations, and fostering a nurturing environment that prioritizes education and development of character. Sonya's story, while unique in its details, offers universal lessons on parenting with faith and a focus on long-term success over immediate gratification.

Now picture Pauline Koch, a very well-educated woman and brilliant pianist. One day, her son came home with a letter from the elementary school he attended. He wasn't able to read the letter, but she told him it said the teachers weren't capable of teaching such a smart child and that one day he'd change the world if given the right education elsewhere. She then bought several books and created a supportive homeschool environment that encouraged her son's intellectual curiosity. Her son, of course, being the one and only Albert Einstein.

How much more impressive it is then that despite not going to school or being able to read, Sonya Carson similarly recognized the transformative power of knowledge. She limited television time and encouraged her sons to read extensively, thereby instilling in them a love for learning. In a similar vein, mothers can follow in the footsteps of Sonya and Pauline by creating a conducive learning environment at home, prioritizing educational activities, and demonstrating the value of knowledge and critical thinking. Encouraging children to explore books, science kits, art supplies, and educational software can turn curiosity into a lifelong passion for learning.

Sonya demonstrated hard work in her daily life, working multiple jobs to support her family and demonstrating unwavering faith in the face of adversity. She set high expectations for her sons, not allowing their circumstances or background to lower their aspirations. She combined these expectations with unconditional love and support, a balance that encouraged her children to strive for excellence without fear of failure.

Recall Albert Einstein, who had a somewhat rocky start to his academic life. He didn't speak until the age of four and didn't read until several years later, leading some to mistakenly believe he wouldn't mount to much. His achievements later in life, dramatically proving these early assessments wrong, underscore the idea that early difficulties don't predestine a child's future capabilities.

Sonya and Pauline celebrated their children's efforts and achievements and provided a safety net of emotional support if and when they stumbled. Sonya encouraged her sons to think independently, always pushing them to look inwards for answers to their problems rather than get someone else to solve them.

An unwavering faith was a cornerstone of Sonya's parenting, providing strength and guidance. While not every family will share the same religious beliefs, incorporating personal or spiritual values into daily life can offer children a sense of purpose and belonging.

Both Ben Carson's and Albert Einstein's stories emphasize the powerful role of parental support, belief, and intervention in helping children overcome challenges and achieve greatness. Just as Pauline Koch did for her son Albert, Sonya Carson and the environment she created for Ben played a critical role in shaping the minds that would go on to change the world. These examples offer invaluable lessons for parents: to nurture their child's unique talents, advocate for their needs, and provide the encouragement and support necessary to help them reach their full potential, no matter the initial obstacles they or you may face.

And in case you're wondering, Albert Einstein read the letter his teacher sent to his mother for the first time after his mother died. He cried as he read the words. His teachers had actually told his mother that he was a badly behaved child that would never amount to anything in his life. How fabulous that she decided in that instant to transform the teacher's words and ultimately transform her son's destiny.

Conclusion

When looking at the lives of these incredible mothers, it's clear they didn't allow things like racial prejudice, being broke, or even their lack of education keep their children from achieving success. They are all maverick mothers in their own right, playing the most important roles in their children's lives. They provided their children with fierce support, influence, and guidance to achieve success.

Seeing just how many of the world's most impactful and influential people had to struggle and overcome ordeals in life is one of the most profound takeaways I had when researching this book. Reading about the horrors the mothers and children had to endure has made me more thankful for the relatively smooth lives my mother, my children, and I have had so far, touch wood!

I'll do my best to summarize key takeaways from this book and separate out different themes based on what the mothers did to raise successful people, whether on purpose or through necessity.

Emotional Support and Security

Mothers who provided a strong emotional foundation for their children managed to form a strong, mutually trusting relationship with them. They were interested and engaged in what went on in their children's lives, making them feel secure. A child who is raised in this way feels like they're always taken care of and will turn to their parents for support. More importantly, a child who was raised with fierce emotional support feels important. They feel like their thoughts and ideas matter, and they can turn to their mother with all of their vulnerabilities and insecurities. They will get useful advice and encouragement in turn, which helps boost their sense of self-worth, which leads to confidence and resilience later in life.

Goldie Hawn is one of many mothers who perfected this craft. She knew the path her daughter Kate was beginning to follow would've led to a less fulfilling life. By actively engaging in her life and guiding her towards an acting career, Goldie helped boost Kate's self-worth and confidence, despite her own anxiety struggles.

Early Learning and Development

Mothers are the child's first teachers. It's the mother who fosters and facilitates language learning, and her interactions with the child contribute to their early cognitive development. Although a lot more goes into children's intellectual growth, the above two skills are crucial for future success in education and communication. Carving out "children's hour" like Ruth Bader Ginsburg did with her daughter is a great example.

But this doesn't mean that the mother has to be highly educated, as is evident in the case of Sonya Carson. Despite only having a third-grade level education, she realized the power that learning and reading can have on a child's life and academic success. Her intervention turned her son's bad report card in fifth grade into huge academic success. He eventually went on to become one of the most successful pediatric neurosurgeons in American history before turning his attention towards a career in politics.

Values and Morals

Mothers who chose to instill core values and morals managed to raise children of fierce integrity and work ethic, as well as an unshakeable character. People raised with a strong moral compass make all the right choices, which has a positive effect on their life and career development. They surround themselves with the right people, choose the best career path, and eventually pursue a career direction that blends things they're passionate about with practical, unique, and inspiring use of their skills. However, for a child to achieve these results, it's necessary for a parent to guide their child's decision-making and teach them the process of weighing pros, cons, and risks against potential benefits. This creates a sort of ethical compass for the child that will serve them throughout their lives.

Baria Alamuddin set an amazing example here. She stood steadfast in her own beliefs and taught her daughters the importance of not only seeing the injustice that is happening around the world but also doing whatever they can to bring human rights to those who aren't allowed them. Her daughter, Amal Clooney, went on to become a highly successful lawyer, fighting social injustice around the world.

Independence and Problem-Solving

Through nurturing and encouragement, maverick mothers go beyond helping children develop essential life skills. They include children in their jobs, trust them with responsibilities, and allow them the independence and freedom to live out experiences that help them exercise their problem-solving abilities. Adult life, particularly a life of devotion and greatness, is bound to come with a unique set of struggles. If a child has well-developed problem-solving skills, they will have mastered a vital asset for success in various aspects of their lives.

Esther Wojcicki is a maternal maverick who allowed her children the freedom to not only solve their own problems but also make mistakes and learn how it feels to fail. She's a firm believer in not coddling a child, something that goes against the helicopter parenting that is practiced by many.

Work Ethic and Perseverance

The mothers in this book all instilled a strong work ethic and the value of perseverance in their children. They did so by setting examples and providing just the right amount of guidance to set their children up for success, yet still allowing enough independence for their children to learn from their own experiences, successes, and failures.

Patricia Noah didn't let laws in her country keep her from achieving her dreams, and she worked hard to provide her son, Trevor, with the best life possible. She cultivated an environment where humor was used to cope with their struggles, which pushed Trevor to become a worldwide comedic phenomenon.

Resilience and Coping Skills

Successful mothers played a role in helping their children develop fierce coping strategies. As you learned, and probably know yourself, parents can only do so much to shelter their children from harm and negativity. Some of the wealthiest people in the world, such as Leonardo DiCaprio, Gary Vaynerchuk, and Elon Musk grew up poor, yet their mothers made sure they were cultured and properly raised, and these women never gave up on supporting their sons to become everything they could be. It meant being involved in their education and training, and including them in family work so that they gained as much experience as they could.

That way, these mavericks taught their children resilience when facing challenges or setbacks. Remember that some of the most accomplished men and women of our time came from humble backgrounds but were raised to do the best they could. With early exposure to work and productivity, they learned how to explore, try various ways of achieving their goals, and learn from their mistakes after failure. These skills proved to be critical for successful people to navigate life's ups and downs and, more importantly, to not allow their current circumstances to limit their imagination and ambitions.

Educational Support

When we say that children need support with education, it means a lot more than the parent simply expressing their appreciation for school and knowledge or expecting the child to have high grades. Supporting children's education means identifying their talents and needs, and then catering to those talents and needs. Most importantly, mothers must be the role models, showing their children the importance of education spending time reading and going to the library rather than watching TV.

Jackie Bezos is a prime example of the importance of being a good educational role model for her children. She was so steadfast in learning and creating the best possible life for her son, Jeff, that she took him with her to the night classes she attended. While raising her children, she continued to study and eventually finished her college qualification at the age of 40 years.

Aspirations and Encouragement

From the time a toddler talks about becoming an astronaut, to when they fashion themselves an operating table to cure their toys, or when they want to do a garage sale, children voice their ambitions loudly. Mothers are the first in line to support those ambitions and make a dedicated effort to facilitate children's ideas toward success. In the examples given in this book, we see that all of the mothers had something in common. Some took longer than others, but they all supported and encouraged their children's ambitions, being a force that lifts them up and not a burden that weighs them down.

Debbie Phelps is one of these maternal mavericks. After realizing that her son, Michael, was struggling at school due to the challenges that his ADHD brought in the classroom, she enrolled him in swimming classes to boost his dopamine levels through exercise, get rid of his high levels of energy, and use his hyperfocus, a common symptom of ADHD, to his advantage in perfecting his swimming technique. He went on to become the most decorated Olympian in American history.

Success Mirrors Success

There is no shortage of career-oriented moms who successfully balanced personal aspirations with parenting, elevating their children's lives in the process. There was no shortage of women who focused on their families, as well, choosing to nurture their children and help them focus on strengths and goals.

As we conclude this exploration of maverick mothers and their world-changing children, it's important to recognize that their influence continues to shape our world. The lessons they've imparted, the values they've instilled, and the examples they've set continue to inspire not just their famous children, but countless others who have been touched by their stories.

Moreover, many of these influential children have become parents themselves, passing on the wisdom and values they learned from their maverick mothers to a new generation. This creates a beautiful continuity, where the positive impact of these remarkable women extends far beyond their immediate families and into the future.

It's also worth noting that while this book has focused on mothers of famously successful individuals, there are countless maverick mothers out there shaping the future in less visible but equally important ways. Every day, mothers around the world are overcoming challenges, breaking barriers, and nurturing the potential in their children. They may not make headlines, but their impact is no less significant.

In the end, perhaps the most powerful lesson from these stories is this: Behind every great achievement, every world-changing innovation, every barrier broken, there's often a mother who believed, who encouraged, who challenged, and who loved unconditionally.

These maverick mothers remind us of the extraordinary power of maternal influence and the amazing impact it can have well beyond the lives of their children.

About the Author

Writing about famous people is way easier than figuring out where my daughter's other shoe went.

Jamie Lillegard

Jamie Lillegard has always wondered how ordinary people end up changing the world. It all started in elementary school when young Jamie learned about Thomas Edison. He was amazed to discover that this world-famous genius was once just a curious kid like him. This sparked a unique hobby in his teenage years when he started making comic books about regular people who develop superpowers based on things other people say to them.

Since earning his degree in computer science, Jamie has worked as a software engineer for some major organizations. But his passion for storytelling and learning about the lives of influential people never left him. He especially enjoys writing about the unseen forces that helped people become successful. Jamie lives in Tampa, Florida, with wife, Louise, and their two daughters.

References

Adventist Review Staff. (2017, November 23). *Sonya Carson, Ben Carson's mother, passes at 88*. Adventist Review. https://adventistreview.org/news/sonya-carson-ben-carsons-mother-passes-at-88/

Ahamed, M. (2022, September 23). *"Felt like the worst mother": Michael Phelps' mom Debbie felt helpless as she kept getting calls regarding his behavior in school*. EssentiallySports. https://www.essentiallysports.com/us-sports-news-swimming-news-felt-like-the-worst-mother-michael-phelps-mom-debbie-felt-helpless-as-she-kept-getting-calls-regarding-his-behavior-in-school/

Alexander, K. L. (2020). *Deloris Jordan*. National Women's History Museum. https://www.womenshistory.org/education-resources/biographies/deloris-jordan

Allen Clark, A. (2008, September 9). *A rare interview with Debbie Phelps*. MomAdvice. https://momadvice.com/post/a-rare-interview-with-debbie-phelps

Amal Clooney. (n.d.). Columbia Law School. https://www.law.columbia.edu/faculty/amal-clooney

Amal Clooney's mother reveals she was advised to abort her due to a placenta condition - Precious Life News. (n.d.). Precious Life. https://preciouslife.com/news/536/amal-clooneys-mother-reveals-she-was-advised-to-abort-her-due-to-a-placenta-condition/

Antoniades, C. B. (2014, December 11). *At home with Debbie Phelps*. Baltimore Magazine. https://www.baltimoremagazine.com/section/homegarden/at-home-with-debbie-phelps/

Arlyn Phoenix biography. (n.d.). JewAge.
https://www.jewage.org/wiki/en/Article:Arlyn_Phoenix_-_Biography

Augustyn, A. (2019). *Michael Jordan | Biography, Stats, & Facts*. In Encyclopædia Britannica.
https://www.britannica.com/biography/Michael-Jordan

Bader Ginsburg, R., Harnett, M., & Williams, W. W. (2016). *My own words*. Simon & Schuster.

Barnes, M. (2017, February 21). *Leah Adler, mother of Steven Spielberg, dies at 97*. The Hollywood Reporter.
https://www.hollywoodreporter.com/news/general-news/leah-adler-dead-mother-steven-spielberg-was-97-978312/

Begg, A. (n.d.). *Judy Murray – "You have to be the parent first."* Working with Parents in Sports.
https://www.parentsinsport.co.uk/2019/04/16/judy-murray-you-have-to-be-the-parent-first/

Bernstein, F. (1990, December 15). *The world is going to hear about this boy*. Fred Bernstein. https://fredbernstein.com/display.php?i=45

Bezos Day One Fund. (n.d.). Bezos Day One Fund.
https://www.bezosdayonefund.org/

Bezos, J. (2017, May 14). *Jeff Bezos' post*. X.
https://twitter.com/JeffBezos/status/863867801181855744?lang=en

Bezos, J. (2022, May 8). *Jeff Bezos's post*. X.
https://twitter.com/JeffBezos/status/1523330938742005760

Bhattacharya, A. (2024, January 18). *Sheryl Sandberg made Meta's board more diverse. Will her departure undo that?* Quartz. https://qz.com/sheryl-sandberg-meta-facebook-board-diversity-1851175311

Billboard Staff. (2016, April 13). *YouTube CEO Susan Wojcicki talks childhood in chat with mom*. Billboard. https://www.billboard.com/pro/youtube-ceo-susan-wojcicki-talks-childhood-in-chat-with-mom/

Branson, R. (2021a, January 11). *Celebrating my mum, Eve Branson*. Virgin. https://www.virgin.com/branson-family/richard-branson-blog/celebrating-my-mum-eve-branson

Branson, R. (2021b, July 15). *Always: a letter to my mum*. Virgin. https://www.virgin.com/branson-family/richard-branson-blog/always-a-letter-to-my-mum

Britannica. (2019). *Jeff Bezos*. In Encyclopædia Britannica. https://www.britannica.com/topic/The-Washington-Post

Bruno Mars. (n.d.). Vogue. https://thevogue.com/artists/bruno-mars/#bio

Bueno, A. (2014, November 12). *Joaquin Phoenix opens up about growing up in the Children of God cult*. ET. https://www.etonline.com/news/153828_joaquin_phoenix_opens_up_about_growing_up_the_children_of_god_cult

Buhr, S. (2017, August 17). *Teen bitcoin millionaire Erik Finman is launching Taylor Swift's '1989' into space*. TechCrunch. https://techcrunch.com/2017/08/17/teen-bitcoin-millionaire-erik-finman-is-launching-taylor-swifts-1989-into-space/

Camargo, M. (2022, June 10). *"I'll happily take her tears of joy." Dwayne Johnson gives his mom the ultimate gift*. InspireMore. https://www.inspiremore.com/ill-happily-take-her-tears-of-joy-dwayne-johnson-gives-his-mom-the-ultimate-gift/

Campbell, Z. (2024, January 18). *How Sheryl Sandberg became the most high-ranking woman in tech*. Mail Online.

https://www.dailymail.co.uk/news/article-12977733/sheryl-sandberg-career-meta-facebook-google.html

Caplan, A. L. (2024, June 13). *Simone Biles' mom is 'Praying that she stays safe' during the gymnast's High-Flying routines.* Peoplemag. https://people.com/simone-biles-mom-praying-she-stays-safe-during-routines-8662953

Carson, B., MD. (2012). *America the beautiful: Rediscovering What Made This Nation Great.* Zondervan.

Carson, B., MD. (1990). *Gifted Hands: The Ben Carson Story.* Review and Herald; Grand Rapids, Michigan.

Carson, B., MD. (2009). *Take the risk: Learning to Identify, Choose, and Live with Acceptable Risk.* Zondervan.

Carson, B., MD. & Carson, C. (2014). *One nation: What We Can All Do to Save America's Future.* Penguin.

Carson, B., MD. & Murphey, C. B. (1992). *Think big : unleashing your potential for excellence.* Zondervan.

Castillo, M. (2017, June 20). *This high school dropout who invested in bitcoin at $12 is now a millionaire at 18.* CNBC. https://www.cnbc.com/2017/06/20/bitcoin-millionaire-erik-finman-says-going-to-college-isnt-worth-it.html

Chiffey, J. (2022, October 4). *Sheryl Sandberg bio: The story of her rise in the tech industry.* Business Chronicler. https://businesschronicler.com/business-bios/sheryl-sandberg-bio/

Chung, G. (2020, December 10). *Sheryl Sandberg opens up about family leave, says women can't "lean in" without "right corporate policies."* People. https://people.com/human-interest/sheryl-sandberg-family-leave-women-cant-lean-in-without-right-corporate-policies/

Clara Hagopian - the real mother of Steve Jobs. (2011, October 25). Media Max. https://mediamax.am/en/news/society/2945/

Clifford, C. (2019, June 14). *Jeff Bezos' single teen mom brought him to night school with her when he was a baby.* CNBC. https://www.cnbc.com/2019/06/14/jeff-bezoss-single-teen-mom-brought-him-to-night-school-with-her.html

Connelly, C. (2018, June 25). *Tom Cruise: Winging it.* Rolling Stone. https://www.rollingstone.com/tv-movies/tv-movie-news/tom-cruise-winging-it-2-190433/

Cook, J. (2011, May 8). *Jeff Bezos' mom: "I knew early on that he was wired a little bit differently."* GeekWire. https://www.geekwire.com/2011/jeff-bezos-mom-i-knew-early-wired-bit-differently/

Corner, L. (2011, July 8). *Rain Phoenix's unusual childhood.* The Guardian. https://www.theguardian.com/lifeandstyle/2011/jul/09/rain-phoenix-river-joaquin-family

Coudriet, C. (2019, June 18). *Want to raise successful kids? Don't make it easy, says mom of YouTube CEO And 23andMe Cofounder.* Forbes. https://www.forbes.com/sites/cartercoudriet/2019/06/18/esther-wojcicki-parenting-susan-anne-janet-women-summit/?sh=38343f215416

Daly, J. (2017, March 20). *The improbable adoption story of Steve Jobs.* Jim Daly. https://jimdaly.focusonthefamily.com/improbable-adoption-story-steve-jobs/

Das, N. (2023, November 23). *Did Joaquin Phoenix grow up in a cult? Exploring his early life amid his movie Napoleon's release.* Pinkvilla. https://www.pinkvilla.com/entertainment/hollywood/did-joaquin-phoenix-grow-up-in-a-cult-exploring-his-early-life-amid-his-movie-napoleons-release-1260484

Dascher, P. P. (2018, May 23). *Dr Ben Carson's mother ~ Sonya Carson ~ Honoring motherhood*. Soul Inspirational Magazine. https://soulmagazine.org/ben-carsons-mother-sonya-carson-honoring-motherhood/

David. (2023, June 7). *Meet Dwayne Johnson's mother Ata Johnson; How is their relationship?* CelebSuburb. https://celebsuburb.com/who-is-ata-johnson-untold-facts-about-dwayne-johnsons-mother/

Day, E. (2014, July 19). *Eve Branson: "I was not saved by Kate Winslet!"* The Guardian. https://www.theguardian.com/theobserver/2014/jul/20/eve-branson-interview

Denison, J. (2015, September 30). *Dr. Ben Carson's mom*. Foundations with Janet Denison. https://www.foundationswithjanet.org/columns/blog-columns/dr-ben-carsons-mom/

Desiree O. (2021, April 15). *The untold truth of Octavia Spencer*. Nicki Swift. https://www.nickiswift.com/384159/the-untold-truth-of-octavia-spencer/

Dodd, S. (2023, August 12). *All about Dwayne Johnson's parents Rocky Johnson and Ata Johnson*. People. https://people.com/all-about-dwayne-johnson-parents-rocky-johnson-ata-johnson-7551148

Eccles, J. S., & Harold, R. D. (1993). *Parent-school involvement during the early adolescent years*. Teachers College Record, 94(3), 568-587.

Eidell, L. (2023, November 13). *All about Jeff Bezos' parents, Jacklyn Bezos, Miguel Bezos and Ted Jorgensen*. People. https://people.com/all-about-jeff-bezos-parents-8384337

Euronews. (2020, March 6). *Journalist Baria Alamuddin discusses women's rights & daughter Amal Clooney*. Euronews.

https://www.euronews.com/2020/03/06/journalist-baria-alamuddin-discusses-women-s-rights-daughter-amal-clooney

Eyewitness News. (2023, February 9). *Leonardo DiCaprio names new snake species after his mother*. ABC7 Los Angeles. https://abc7.com/leonardo-dicaprio-new-snake-species-irmelin-indenbirken-sibon-irmelindicaprioae/12789555/

Fairygodboss.com. (n.d.). *On behalf of working moms, Sheryl Sandberg told the US government what's up*. Ellevate. https://www.ellevatenetwork.com/articles/8235-on-behalf-of-working-moms-sheryl-sandberg-told-the-us-government-what-s-up

Feloni, R. (2016, November 16). *Richard Branson explains the most important lesson he learned from his mom — and it included being pushed out of the car at age 6*. Business Insider. https://www.businessinsider.com/richard-branson-mom-taught-him-take-risks-2016-11

Ferguson, D. (2015, November 20). *Judy Murray: my family values*. The Guardian. https://www.theguardian.com/lifeandstyle/2015/nov/20/judy-murray-my-family-values-andy-murray-jamie-murray

Fetch! Pet Care. (2015, December 17). *Dwayne Johnson Pays For Doomed Dog's Surgery*. https://fetchpetcare.com/blog/dwayne-johnson-pays-for-doomed-dogs-surgery/

Fishburne, M., JD. (2018, March 9). *Raising an inventor*. https://www.linkedin.com/pulse/raising-inventor-michelle-fishburne-lewis

Fleming, K. (2023, April 3). *What Michael Jordan and "Air" reveal about parenting*. New York Post. https://nypost.com/2023/04/03/air-why-michael-jordan-can-fly-and-hem-pants-too/

Foster, K. (2022, May 15). *Judy Murray left "disgusted" after a man put a hand down her trousers.* Mail Online. https://www.dailymail.co.uk/news/article-10818987/Judy-Murray-left-disgusted-drunk-man-hand-trousers-event.html

Foster, T. (2020, May 3). *10 things you didn't know about Amal Clooney.* TVovermind. https://tvovermind.com/10-things-you-didnt-know-about-amal-clooney/

Fox, E. J. (2015, October 21). *How Elon Musk's Mom (and her Twin Sister) Raised the First Family of Tech.* Vanity Fair. https://www.vanityfair.com/news/2015/10/elon-musk-family-maye-musk

Garner, G. (2022, May 8). *Sheryl Sandberg honors her mom, soon-to-be mother-in-law, and late husband's mother for mother's day.* People. https://people.com/human-interest/sheryl-sandberg-pays-tribute-all-the-amazing-moms-her-life-mothers-day/

Gaur, A. (2023, June 28). *"Stuck at home with these two little..." - British legend Andy Murray's mother discloses the problematic parental fact that motivated her to pursue tennis coaching.* EssentiallySports. https://www.essentiallysports.com/atp-tennis-news-stuck-at-home-with-these-two-little-british-legend-andy-murrays-mother-discloses-the-problematic-parental-fact-that-motivated-her-to-pursue-tennis-coaching/

Gebreyes, R. (2016, November 22). *How immigrant roots made Sheryl Sandberg's parents who they are today.* Huffington Post. https://www.huffpost.com/entry/sheryl-sandberg-parents-talk-to-me_n_58334346e4b058ce7aac5171

Guglielmi, J. (2018, February 16). *How Octavia Spencer's mom inspired her success: "I am a product of her disadvantages."* Yahoo Entertainment. https://www.yahoo.com/entertainment/octavia-spencer-mom-inspired-her-185811747.html

Harder, C. (2022, October 31). *The no. 1 piece of parenting advice from a mom who raised CEOs.* Today's Parent. https://www.todaysparent.com/family/parenting/parenting-advice-esther-wojcicki/

Harlow, P. (2016, November 2). *Why YouTube's chief wants parents to take more time off.* CNNMoney. https://money.cnn.com/2016/11/02/technology/susan-wojcicki-parental-leave/index.html

Hetzner, C. (2024, May 7). *Elon Musk blasts obsolete education system for failing to reach kids—'you don't want a teacher in front of a board'.* Fortune. https://fortune.com/2024/05/07/elon-musk-tesla-education-teaching-interactive-entertainment-children/

Hewitt, C. (2021, March 6). *How Tom Cruise got Hollywood moving again during the pandemic.* Empire Online. https://www.empireonline.com/movies/features/how-tom-cruise-got-hollywood-moving-again-during-the-pandemic-world-exclusive/

Heyman, J. D. (2017, February 13). *Tom Cruise's mother, Mary Lee South, dies.* People. https://people.com/celebrity/tom-cruises-mother-mary-lee-south-dies/

HuffPost. (2016, April 16). *#TalkToMe: Susan & Esther Wojcicki* [Video]. YouTube. https://www.youtube.com/watch?v=H6NlBNGFa9w&t=429s

Ignatius, A. (2023, February 2). *ActOne Group founder Janice Bryant Howroyd: Never compromise your values in a quest to succeed.* Harvard Business Review. https://hbr.org/2023/02/actone-group-founder-janice-bryant-howroyd-never-compromise-your-values-in-a-quest-to-succeed

Influence Watch. (2024, February 19). *Bezos Family Foundation (BFF) - InfluenceWatch.* InfluenceWatch. https://www.influencewatch.org/non-profit/bezos-family-foundation-bff/

Jain, M. (2022, June 14). *"When my father died…"- Michael Phelps' mother opens up on her difficult childhood*. EssentiallySports. https://www.essentiallysports.com/us-sports-news-swimming-news-when-my-father-died-michael-phelps-mother-opens-up-on-her-difficult-childhood/

Jones, C. (2023, September 12). *Elon Musk was bullied so badly he was hospitalized and forced to move schools*. The Mirror. https://www.mirror.co.uk/news/us-news/elon-musk-bullied-badly-hospitalised-30919374

Jones, J. (2024, May 12). *Kevin Durant's NBA MVP speech 10 years ago remains the classic Mother's Day gift*. The Athletic. https://www.nytimes.com/athletic/5481384/2024/05/12/kevin-durant-the-real-mvp-wanda-durant/#

Jones, T. (2023, October 13). *Gary Vaynerchuk recalls "best" childhood growing up "poor."* Page Six. https://pagesix.com/2023/10/13/gary-vaynerchuk-recalls-best-childhood-growing-up-poor/

Jordan, D., & Lewis, G. (1996). *Family first: winning the parenting game*. Harpersanfrancisco.

Jordan, D., Jordan, R. M., & Evans, S. W. (2004). *Did I tell you I love you today?* Simon & Schuster Books for Young Readers.

Jordan, D., Jordan, R. M., & Nelson, K. (2003). *Salt in his shoes: Michael Jordan in pursuit of a dream*. Simon & Schuster Books for Young Readers.

Jordan, M. (n.d.). *A quote by Michael Jordan*. Good Reads. https://www.goodreads.com/quotes/281891-my-mother-is-my-root-my-foundation-she-planted-the

Juneau, J., & Huver, S. (2022, April 22). *Steven Spielberg on how "E.T." was inspired by his parents' divorce: "We all take care of each other."* People. https://people.com/movies/steven-spielberg-says-et-was-inspired-by-his-parents-divorce/

Junod, T. (2012, November 15). *Elon Musk: Triumph of his will*. Esquire. https://www.esquire.com/news-politics/a16681/elon-musk-interview-1212/

Kerkhof, R. (2023, August 17). *Trevor Noah's mom: Meet Patricia Noah the strong woman behind the world famous comedian.* https://www.blinkist.com/magazine/posts/trevor-noahs-mom-meet-patricia-noah

Kher, T. (2024, June 2). *Michael Jordan once donated millions for students influenced by his mother, Deloris Jordan.* The SportsRush. https://thesportsrush.com/nba-news-11-years-after-retiring-michael-jordan-began-dropping-millions-on-students-because-of-his-mother-deloris-jordan/

Kim, W. (2023, January 27). *What does it mean to give away a $118 billion fortune?* Vox. https://www.vox.com/recode/23553730/jeff-bezos-philanthropy-giving-pledge-charity#

Kimble, L. (2017, January 30). *Bruno Mars on mother's death: "Half your heart goes away."* People. https://people.com/music/bruno-mars-talks-mother-death-latina/

Koehler, S., & Paris, S. (2023, May 4). *The untold truth of Joaquin Phoenix.* Looper. https://www.looper.com/167662/the-untold-truth-of-joaquin-phoenix/

Kroll, L. (2011, October 6). *Sean Parker's Tribute To His Hero Steve Jobs.* Forbes. https://www.forbes.com/sites/luisakroll/2011/10/06/sean-parkers-tribute-to-his-hero-steve-jobs/?sh=6a3b02827ae0

Kubota, S. (2023, February 3). *Dwayne Johnson reveals his mom was in a serious car crash.* Today. https://www.today.com/popculture/dwayne-johnson-reveals-mom-was-serious-car-crash-rcna68946

Kumawat, N. (2023, December 12). *Were Dwayne "The Rock" Johnson's parents wrestlers too? All you need to know about Rocky and Ata Johnson.*

Pinkvilla. https://www.pinkvilla.com/sports/were-dwayne-the-rock-johnsons-parents-wrestlers-too-all-you-need-to-know-about-rocky-and-ata-johnson-1264776

Langston, K. (2023, November 24). *All about Steven Spielberg's parents, Arnold Spielberg and Leah Adler*. People. https://people.com/all-about-arnold-spielberg-leah-adler-steven-spielberg-parents-7566940

Lemire, S. (2023, March 20). *Goldie Hawn's message to parents: "Listen to your children."* Today. https://www.today.com/popculture/news/goldie-hawn-women-of-the-year-usa-today-rcna75467

Leskin, P., & Jackson, S. (2023, February 16). *The career rise of Susan Wojcicki, who rented her garage to Google's founders in 1998 and is now stepping down as the CEO of YouTube*. Business Insider. https://www.businessinsider.com/susan-wojcicki-youtube-ceo-bio-career-life-2018-12

Libbey, D. (2023, April 11). *Miles Teller Calls Out Tom Cruise's Top Gun: Maverick Oscars Snub: 'We Don't Realize How Much Work And Effort Goes Into That'*. Yahoo Entertainment. https://www.yahoo.com/entertainment/miles-teller-calls-tom-cruise-191638870.html

Liwag Dixon, C., & Ledford, B. (2023, January 30). *The untold truth of Bruno Mars*. The List. https://www.thelist.com/83646/untold-truth-bruno-mars/

Luscombe, B. (2015, August 27). *Meet YouTube's view master*. Time. https://time.com/4012832/meet-youtubes-view-master/

Madell, R. (2021, June 15). *A 22-year-old bitcoin multimillionaire shares how he spends his money after dropping out of high school*. Business Insider. https://www.businessinsider.com/22-year-old-bitcoin-multimillionaire-how-spends-money-2021-6

Malik, M. (2023, March 20). *Who is Amal Clooney's sister, Tala Alamuddin?* Grazia Middle East. https://graziamagazine.com/me/articles/amal-clooneys-sister-tala-alamuddin/

Marquina, S. (2017, July 21). *Charlize Theron Recalls the Night Her Mom Killed Her Alcoholic Father.* Us Weekly. https://www.usmagazine.com/celebrity-news/news/charlize-theron-recalls-the-night-her-mom-killed-her-alcoholic-father-w493603/

Maye Musk: a Canadian grandparent. (2023, September 23). Canadian Grandparents. https://canadiangrandparents.ca/maye-musk-a-canadian-grandparent/

McArdle, T., & Gauk-Roger, T. (2023, January 6). *Steven Spielberg dedicates award to late parents: "They're holding hands across the stars right now."* People. https://people.com/movies/steven-spielberg-dedicates-award-to-late-parents-theyre-holding-hands-across-the-stars-right-now/

McElwee, M. (2023, July 14). *Judy Murray: "I knew I wasn't OK" – my mental turmoil at being a tennis mother.* The Telegraph. https://www.telegraph.co.uk/tennis/2023/07/14/judy-murray-andy-murray-on-tennis-mom-mental-turmoil/

McLoughlin, L. (2023, November 3). *Charlize Theron reflects on "trauma" of her mum fatally shooting her father.* Evening Standard. https://www.standard.co.uk/showbiz/charlize-theron-mother-fatally-shooting-father-self-defence-b1117975.html

McRae, D. (2014, June 16). *Judy Murray on the Dunblane massacre: "I just left the car and ran."* The Guardian. https://www.theguardian.com/sport/2014/jun/17/judy-murray-dunblane-massacre-just-left-car-and-ran

Medina, M. (2019, March 7). *LeBron James talks about Michael Jordan's influence on his career.* USA Today. https://eu.usatoday.com/story/sports/nba/2019/03/07/lebron-james-michael-jordan-lakers/39160245/

Michael Phelps' mom to head Education Foundation Debbie Phelps brings 40 years of educator experience. (2012, October 11). WBALTV. https://www.wbaltv.com/article/michael-phelps-mom-to-head-education-foundation-1/7077082

Miller, A. (2016, December 8). *James Island native and NFL star Roddy White credits his biggest fan for where he is today.* Post and Courier. https://www.postandcourier.com/sports/james-island-native-and-nfl-star-roddy-white-credits-his-biggest-fan-for-where-he/article_ed0cb583-d68c-5d57-89a2-ced687d6626e.html

Moorhead, J. (2017, June 1). *Judy Murray: I'm not a pushy parent.* Family | the Guardian. https://amp.theguardian.com/lifeandstyle/2011/oct/15/andy-murray-judy-jamie-tennis

Murphy, B. (2021, June 29). *Want to raise successful kids? Elon Musk's mom says this one habit matters most (most parents do the opposite).* Inc.Africa. https://www.incafrica.com/article/bill-murphy-jr-want-to-raise-successful-kids-elon-musks-mom-says-this-1-habit-matters-most-most-parents-do-opposite/

Murray, T. (2023, January 23). *Jennifer Connelly thinks Tom Cruise 'absolutely deserves' an Oscar nomination for Top Gun: Maverick.* The Independent. https://www.independent.co.uk/arts-entertainment/films/news/jennifer-connelly-tom-cruise-oscar-top-gun-maverick-b2267766.html#

Nath, S. (2022, March 15). *Dwayne Johnson reveals the advice his mother gave him that made him the gentleman he is today.* EssentiallySports. https://www.essentiallysports.com/wwe-news-dwayne-johnson-reveals-the-advice-his-mother-gave-him-that-made-him-the-gentleman-he-is-today/

Noah, T. (2016). *Born a crime: Stories from a South African childhood.* Spiegel & Grau.

Noah, T. (n.d.). *Social investor – born an optimist.* https://www.chandlerfoundation.org/social-investor/born-an-optimist

Oard, B. (2023, August 25). *River Phoenix's mom posts bday tribute to the late actor on Instagram.* Mail Online. https://www.dailymail.co.uk/tvshowbiz/joaquin-phoenix/article-12443547/Arlyn-Heart-Phoenix-pays-tribute-late-son-River-Phoenix-Instagram-actors-53rd-birthday.html

Ogden, G. (2016, December 14). *Gerard Butler: "Stop Taking Yourself So Damn Seriously".* Coachmaguk. https://www.coachweb.com/entertainment/6129/gerard-butler-stop-taking-yourself-so-damn-seriously

Octavia Spencer: I had a very strong mother. (2016, December 22). The Times of India. https://timesofindia.indiatimes.com/octavia-spencer-i-had-a-very-strong-mother/articleshow/56118435.cms?from=mdr

Palmeri, S. (2023, December 1). *How Tom Cruise kept his family afloat when his mother finally left his abusive father.* Goalcast. https://www.goalcast.com/tom-cruise-family-abusive-father/

Paul, C. (2023, November 3). *Every noble cause $800M Dwayne Johnson has supported since becoming a global phenomenon.* EssentiallySports. https://www.essentiallysports.com/wwe-news-every-noble-cause-eight-hundred-million-worth-dwayne-johnson-has-supported-since-becoming-a-global-phenomenon/

Paz, Z. (2020, December 10). *Michael Phelps facts and his learning disability.* LD Resources Foundation. https://www.ldrfa.org/michael-phelps/

Penn, A. (2019, October 5). *Trevor Noah's mom: The extraordinary life of Patricia Noah.* Shortform Books. https://www.shortform.com/blog/trevor-noah-mom/

Perry, T. (2023, November 15). *Mother of successful daughters shares her secret.* Upworthy. https://www.upworthy.com/ceo-mom-unpopular-parenting-rule-rp3

Petit, S. (2016, December 21). *Octavia Spencer opens up about losing her mother.* People. https://people.com/movies/octavia-spencer-losing-mother-18-lessons/

Picou, S. (2024, July 22). *Ruth Bader Ginsburg's 2 Children: All About Jane and James.* Peoplemag. https://people.com/all-about-ruth-bader-ginsburg-kids-8649543

Poirier-Leroy, O. (2018, March 31). *Michael Phelps' mom on how to raise an Olympian.* Your Swim Book. https://www.yourswimlog.com/michael-phelps-mom-on-how-to-raise-an-olympian/

PSN Team. (2017, May 17). *Debbie Phelps shares some of her life lessons.* Parenting Special Needs. https://www.parentingspecialneeds.org/article/debbie-phelps-life-lessons/2/

Puente, M. (2017, February 13). *Tom Cruise's mother dies, age 80.* USA Today. https://www.usatoday.com/story/life/movies/2017/02/13/tom-cruises-mother-dies-age-80/97872176/

Quihuiz, A. (2023a, April 5). *All about Michael Jordan's parents, Deloris and James R. Jordan, Sr.* People. https://people.com/sports/all-about-deloris-jordan-james-r-jordan-michael-jordan-parents/

Quihuiz, A. (2023b, July 25). *All about Leonardo DiCaprio's parents, George DiCaprio and Irmelin Indenbirken.* People. https://people.com/all-about-leonardo-dicaprio-parents-george-dicaprio-irmelin-indenbirken-7502510

RandyW. (2010, January 15). *Dwayne "The Rock" Johnsons mom cancer free!!* Lung Cancer Support Community.

https://forums.lungevity.org/topic/37483-dwayne-the-rock-johnsons-mom-cancer-free/

Remembering Eve Branson. (n.d.). Virgin Atlantic. https://flywith.virginatlantic.com/za/en/stories/remembering-eve-branson-on-mothers-day.html

Rossi, R. (2017, January 16). *Octavia Spencer treats low-income families to free screening of "Hidden Figures."* TheWrap. https://www.thewrap.com/octavia-spencer-treated-low-income-families-to-free-screening-of-hidden-figures/

Ryzik, M. (2018, December 27). *Bringing to Life the Ruth Bader Ginsburg Only Her Family Knows.* The New York Times. https://www.nytimes.com/2018/12/27/movies/on-the-basis-of-sex-ruth-bader-ginsburg.html

Samakow, J. (2013, May 7). *Sheryl Sandberg's words about her mother might surprise you.* HuffPost. https://www.huffpost.com/entry/adele-sandberg-sheryl-sandberg-mom-tribute_n_3230540

Sandberg, S. (2016, May 6). *Sheryl Sandberg post.* Facebook. https://www.facebook.com/sheryl

Sanwari, A. (2022, December 8). *Kate Hudson reveals the unexpected way that Goldie Hawn shaped her career.* Hello! https://www.hellomagazine.com/healthandbeauty/mother-and-baby/20221208159175/kate-hudson-reveals-goldie-hawn-unwelcome-decision-changed-her-life/

Scarsella, J. (2024, March 21). *Michael Phelps Foundation teaches kids the stroke of success.* The Business Download. https://thebusinessdownload.com/michael-phelps-foundation-teaches-kids-the-stroke-of-success/

Schama, C. (2022, February 5). *Ruth Bader Ginsburg: Hero for pregnant women.* ELLE. https://www.elle.com/culture/career-politics/news/a31721/ruth-bader-ginsburg-hero-for-pregnant-women/

Seejal. (2024, January 8). *Tom Cruise's mother Mary Lee Pfeiffer's shocking claims.* Biography Gist. https://biographygist.com/tom-cruises-mother-mary-lee-pfeiffers-shocking-claims/

Shahid. (2016, January 6). *Baria Alamuddin, mother of Amal Clooney: her age, details!* Married Biography. https://marriedbiography.com/baria-alamuddin-mother-amal-clooney-age-childhood-parents-career-relationships-wiki/

Shen, F. (2019, March 5). *Professor Jane Ginsburg reflects on her family history as "On the Basis of Sex" screens at Athena Film Festival.* Columbia Daily Spectator. https://www.columbiaspectator.com/arts-and-entertainment/2019/03/05/professor-jane-ginsburg-reflects-on-her-family-history-as-on-the-basis-of-sex-screens-at-athena-film-festival/

Sheridan, E., & Carneiro, B. (2013, June 3). *Singer Bruno Mars' mother Bernadette Hernandez, 55, "dies of brain aneurysm."* Mail Online. https://www.dailymail.co.uk/tvshowbiz/article-2334649/Bruno-Mars-mother-Bernadette-Hernandez-55-dies-brain-aneurysm.html

Sherman, M. (2021, December 10). *11 Times Leonardo DiCaprio Tried to Save the World.* Netflix. https://www.netflix.com/tudum/articles/dont-look-up-netflix-leo-dicaprio-saved-the-world

Solutions, R. (2023, September 11). *Tackling gender injustice head on.* Clooney Foundation for Justice. https://cfj.org/news/tackling-gender-injustice-head-on/

Stevenson, R. (2021, April 27). *Steve Jobs: The childhood of a great inventor.* BBC Science Focus Magazine. https://www.sciencefocus.com/future-technology/steve-jobs-the-childhood-of-a-great-inventor

Strauss, V. (2011, October 5). *Steve Jobs told students: "Stay hungry. Stay foolish."* Washington Post.

https://www.washingtonpost.com/blogs/answer-sheet/post/steve-jobs-told-students-stay-hungry-stay-foolish/2011/10/05/gIQA1qVjOL_blog.html

Teamgaryvee. (2020, September 3). *Everything you wanted to know about Gary Vaynerchuk*. Gary Vaynerchuk. https://garyvaynerchuk.com/everything-you-wanted-to-know-about-gary-vaynerchuk/

Tocino, K. (2016, October 17). *Did you know that Bruno Mars' mother was a Bayot?* Y101fm. https://www.y101fm.com/features/lifestyle/entertainment/4440-did-you-know-that-bruno-mars-mother-was-a-bayot

Todisco, E. (2019, May 2). *Goldie Hawn reflects on her childhood anxiety— and how meditation helped her find happiness again*. People. https://people.com/movies/goldie-hawn-opens-up-about-her-childhood-anxiety-and-how-meditation-helped-her-find-happiness-again/

Todisco, E. (2021, January 26). *Elon Musk's mom Maye knew he was a genius at age 3*. People. https://people.com/human-interest/elon-musk-mom-maye-knew-son-genius-3-years-old/

Totenberg, N. (2020, September 18). *Justice Ruth Bader Ginsburg, champion of gender equality, dies at 87*. NPR. https://www.npr.org/2020/09/18/100306972/justice-ruth-bader-ginsburg-champion-of-gender-equality-dies-at-87

Tremaine, J. (2023, August 1). *All about Elon Musk's mother Maye Musk*. People. https://people.com/all-about-elon-musk-mother-maye-musk-7502182

United Hatzalah. (2021, December 28). *Amy Korenvaes, Joel and Adele Sandberg, Sheryl Sandberg and Jennifer Attias - Miami Gala 2021* [Video]. YouTube. https://www.youtube.com/watch?v=dPGaAwmxhjA

VanHoose, B. (2022, November 2). *Steven Spielberg says his parents were "nagging" him to make movie about them before their deaths.* People. https://people.com/movies/steven-spielberg-late-parents-nagged-him-to-make-movie-about-them/

Vaynerchuk, G. (2016, May 8). *For Tamara and all the other amazing mothers out there.* Gary Vaynerchuk. https://garyvaynerchuk.com/for-tamara-and-all-the-other-moms/

Vogue. (2024, March 15). *Jeff Bezos and Lauren Sanchez gave out $100 million at last night's Bezos Courage & Civility Awards.* Vogue. https://www.vogue.com/slideshow/inside-the-bezos-courage-and-civility-awards-2024

Wabwile, A. (2023, November 2). *Facts about Jacklyn Bezos: Jeff Bezos' mother's billionaire lifestyle.* Briefly. https://briefly.co.za/facts-lifehacks/celebrities-biographies/172344-facts-jacklyn-bezos-jeff-bezos-mother-billionaire-lifestyle/

Wallace, D. (2023, January 10). *Steven Spielberg's mother predicted his success when he was still a kid making movies in the family kitchen.* Parade. https://parade.com/celebrities/steven-spielberg-mother-leah-adler

Weaver, E. (2023, December 20). *All about Trevor Noah's parents, Patricia and Robert Noah.* People. https://people.com/all-about-trevor-noah-parents-8416111

Weaver, E. (2024, January 11). *All about Kurt Russell and Goldie Hawn's 4 kids.* People. https://people.com/parents/all-about-kurt-russell-goldie-hawn-kids/

Weinberg, L. (2022, October 1). *Why Kate Hudson isn't trying to emulate mom Goldie Hawn's career.* E! Online. https://www.eonline.com/news/1348724/why-kate-hudson-isnt-trying-to-emulate-mom-goldie-hawns-career

Whitman, S. (2022, May 4). *Leonardo DiCaprio's mom: Everything to know about Irmelin Indenbirken.* Hollywood Life. https://hollywoodlife.com/feature/leonardo-dicaprio-mom-4725193/

Who is The Rock's mom, Ata Johnson? (n.d.). Sportskeeda. https://www.sportskeeda.com/wwe/the-rock-mom

Who was Mary Lee Pfeiffer? (2020, June 18). CelebAnswers. https://celebanswers.com/who-was-mary-lee-pfeiffer/

Wickham, E. (2017, March 6). *5 amazing things Michael Phelps said about his mom.* SwimSwam. https://swimswam.com/5-amazing-things-michael-phelps-said-mom/

Wilson, E. (2023, July 7). *Inside Judy Murray's life – rocky romances, tennis career and fears for son Andy.* The Mirror. https://www.mirror.co.uk/3am/celebrity-news/inside-judy-murrays-life--30412695

Wojcicki, E. (2019). *How to raise successful people: Simple lessons for radical results.* Hutchinson.

Wojcicki, E. (2022, December 16). *I raised 2 successful CEOs and a doctor—here's the parenting style I never used on my kids.* CNBC. https://www.cnbc.com/2022/09/17/i-raised-2-successful-ceos-and-a-doctor-here-is-the-worst-parenting-style-that-harms-kids.html

Wood, R. (2016, March 6). *#ASKGARYVEE. An Interview With Gary Vaynerchuk.* Top Agents Playbook. https://www.topagentsplaybook.com/podcast/tap-39-askgaryvee-an-interview-with-gary-vaynerchuk/

Woodard, J. L. (2014, April 22). *Med student meets Ben Carson, neurosurgeon who inspired him.* Clarion Ledger. https://eu.clarionledger.com/story/news/2014/04/22/med-student-meets-ben-carson-neurosurgeon-inspired-life/8026259/

Zachareck, S. (2022, November 16). *This is Steven Spielberg like you've never seen him before.* Time. https://time.com/6234045/steven-spielberg-interview-the-fabelmans/

www.ingramcontent.com/pod-product-compliance
Lightning Source LLC
LaVergne TN
LVHW040050080526
838202LV00045B/3562